James Blackwood
Memories

James Blackwood Memories

by

Some of His Best Friends

*Compiled and Edited
with an Introduction by*
Allen Dennis

With Personal Reflections by
James Blackwood

QUAIL RIDGE PRESS

QUAIL RIDGE PRESS
P. O. Box 123 / Brandon, MS 39043
1-800-343-1583

Library of Congress Cataloging-in-Publication Data

James Blackwood memories / by some of his best friends;
  compiled and edited with an introduction by Allen
  Dennis; reflections by James Blackwood.
     p.   cm.
   ISBN 0-937552-79-8
   1. Blackwood, James, vocalist--Appreciation. 2.
   Blackwood Brothers Quartet.   I. Dennis, Allen.
   ML420.B6335J36   1997
   782.25' 4' 092--dc21
   [B]   96-6611
                                                CIP
                                                 MN

All photographs in this book are from the collections of James
Blackwood and Allen Dennis, or were furnished by the con-
tributors.

In Loving Memory of:

DOYLE BLACKWOOD
(1911-1974)

R. W. BLACKWOOD
(1921-1954)

ROY BLACKWOOD
(1900-1971)

NEIL DENNIS
(1917-1995)

BILL LYLES
(1921-1954)

Contents

   I. Personnel of The Blackwood Brothers Quartet

  II. Major Awards Won by James Blackwood

 III. James Blackwood's "Top Ten"

 IV. James' Itinerary for 1997

Introduction

by
Allen Dennis

When I was growing up in the hills of East Tennessee in the 1950s, my Daddy and I shared several cherished traditions. For example, we loved Tennessee football and hoped that Ole Miss never won another game; we were Yankee fans and hated the Dodgers; country ham and fried okra constituted a gourmet meal; and we loved Southern gospel music.

Daddy and I hunted a great deal during the 1950s. Usually we hunted crows, which flocked by the hundreds of thousands to grain fields near Englewood and Etowah. Toward evening, they would head toward their roosts, and my Daddy and I would trail them along the narrow dirt roads, stopping every now and then to take cover in a pine thicket and blast down a few. As we tracked our quarry, we would listen to radio station WLAR in Athens as George Mooney, the voice of Tennessee football, extolled the exploits of heroes such as Tommy Bronson, Bill Anderson, and Johnny Majors.

As dusk began to fall and we started the long drive back home to Athens, we had another tradition. We would tune our radio to WDEH ("the Mighty Voice of the Sweetwater Valley") in Sweetwater, Tennessee. At about five o'clock on Saturday afternoons, WDEH would play Southern gospel music. Our favorites were The Blackwood Brothers (*Give the World a Smile* and *I'll Meet You In the Morning*) and The Chuckwagon Gang (*There is Glory on the Winning Side* and *A Beautiful Life*). We would pat our feet and sing along until we got home. It was always the perfect ending to a day of hunting and Tennessee football. Through the years since then, Southern gospel music has been dear to me, both because I love it and because it brings back fond memories of the wonderful times my Daddy (who passed away in November, 1995) and I had together.

From time to time in the years since, I had the opportunity to see The Blackwood Brothers in concert and let them stir afresh the warm feelings associated with their singing. Little did I dream that one day I would get to meet James Blackwood, and it *never* occurred to me that he would become my friend.

But let's cut to the 1990s. In 1992, the Mississippi Humanities Council inaugurated a series of programs known as Chautauqua presentations. In the Chautauqua format, scholars or knowledgeable persons in the humanities portray famous figures from the past in full costume and in the first person. The presenter gives a monologue as the figure, and then answers questions from the audience while remaining "in character." In the latter portion of the performance, the presenter "breaks character" and answers questions *about* the figure he has just impersonated.

In the 1992 Mississippi Chautauqua program, I portrayed Abraham Lincoln in several presentations throughout Mississippi from Iuka to Gulfport. Other characters presented in that Chautauqua were women journalists Pearl Rivers and Ida B. Wells, and Confederate President Jefferson Davis. Another successful Mississippi Chautauqua followed in 1993, presenting the characters of Theodore G. Bilbo, Fannie Lou Hamer, and Greenwood LeFlore.

In late 1993, Dr. Cora Norman, Executive Director of the Mississippi Humanities Council, asked me if I would develop a proposal for the 1994-95 Chautauqua presentation. Almost immediately, I decided to create a Chautauqua based on famous Mississippi musical figures. Mississippi's musical heritage is so rich that it was difficult for me to decide which characters to include. Eventually, I selected the father of country music, Jimmie Rodgers, the noted 19th-century African-American diva Elizabeth Taylor Greenfield, and the greatest baritone in the history of Southern gospel music, R. W. Blackwood. A prerequisite for selection was that the figure had to be a native Mississippian and be deceased; Jimmie Rodgers was from Meridian, Elizabeth Greenfield was from Natchez, and R. W. Blackwood was from Choctaw County near Ackerman.

Now, my task was to find scholars who could present historical information about these characters as well as sing (in a reasonably acceptable fashion!) some of their songs. Dr. Sammy Cranford, Professor of History at Delta State University, agreed to portray Jimmie Rodgers, while Dr. Ellistine Holly, Professor of Music at Jackson State University, took on the role of Elizabeth Taylor Greenfield. Finding someone to portray R. W. Blackwood proved to be a more formidable task.

In November, 1993, I called Chrissy Wilson at the Mississippi Department of Archives and History to ask for her suggestions. I knew that Chrissy had put together an impressive collection of Blackwood Brothers photographs for display at the Archives, and I thought that in her research she might have come in contact with a Blackwood Brothers scholar who would be interested in portraying R. W. She replied that she did not know of anyone, but that she had James Blackwood's telephone number. "You've got *James Blackwood's* telephone number?" I exclaimed in disbelief that one of my boyhood idols could be so accessible.

11

Less than 10 minutes later, I was actually talking to James Blackwood on the telephone. I explained the reason for my call, and James (who was "Mr. Blackwood" to me at that time) told me that he would think about it and let me know if he could think of anyone who could portray R. W.

During the next few months, one "R. W." lead after another proved to be fruitless. Also, my dear friend Sammy Cranford died suddenly in February, 1994, leaving a void not only in the Chautauqua presentation but in my life. Mississippi Chautauqua 1994 seemed to be jinxed. Ellistine had agreed to portray Elizabeth Greenfield, but the roles of Jimmie Rodgers and R. W. Blackwood remained to be filled.

Meanwhile, James and I had become acquaintances. My fianceé and I arranged to meet him at a restaurant in Memphis, where we both acted like teenage groupies in the presence of our idol. Brenda even knocked over her tea glass in her nervousness, drenching James' side of the table. Yet, from this inauspicious beginning has grown warm friendship.

In the late spring of 1994, I decided that I would portray Jimmie Rodgers in the 1994-95 Chautauqua. My singing and guitar ability were not comparable to Sammy Cranford's, but time was slipping by. I still had found no one to portray R. W. Blackwood, and I was getting desperate since our first performances were scheduled for November.

Sometime in early August when I was driving home from my office, the thought hit me that I should ask James to portray R.W. Although James was not a trained academician (usually one of the requirements for a Chautauqua performer), no one anywhere could possibly know more about R. W. Blackwood. Certainly no one could sing R. W.'s songs any better. So, I called James with my proposal. He was just about to leave on tour with The James Blackwood Quartet, so I told him to think about it during the tour, and to let me know when he returned.

About two weeks later, James called to say that he would indeed portray R. W. Blackwood. I was ecstatic. Not only had I found the best possible person to portray the legendary baritone, but this meant that *I* would get to travel and perform with James Blackwood! Dreams do come true!

Over the next sixteen months, James, Ellistine, and I performed Mississippi Chautauqua 1994-1995 in Gulfport, Picayune, Cleveland, Tupelo, and twice in Jackson. As R. W., James usually sang *He Bought My Soul at Calvary* and *I Believe*. On one or two occasions when time permitted, he also performed *I Want to be More Like Jesus*. Two of these

Allen Dennis, Brenda Dennis, Ellistine Holly, James Blackwood, and Mim Blackwood at Mary Mahoney's Restaurant in Biloxi, Mississippi, after a performance of Mississippi Chautauqua 1994-1995 in Gulfport.

---

performances were particularly significant, for it was difficult for James to portray R. W. without being deeply moved. As long as James was singing, he was fine; but he often choked up when describing (as R. W.) the last concert The Blackwood Brothers gave before the fatal plane crash of June 30, 1954.

Our first Chautauqua presentation was in Gulfport in early November, 1994. There was something almost supernatural about that performance, for Gulfport was the site of the final Blackwood Brothers concert on June 29 before R. W. and Bill Lyles were killed near Clanton, Alabama, the next day. I know James sensed the deep irony of that occasion.

About two weeks later, we presented our program at the Old Capitol in Jackson. The presence of Bill Lyles' widow, Ruth Lyles Jeffers, and R.W.'s sister-in-law, Yvonne Denson, at this performance made it even more difficult for James to stay "in character" as R. W. When James' voice began to crack near the end of his presentation, there was absolutely not a dry eye in the house. I have often wished that Bill Gaither could have been there with his video crew to capture that moment. As moving as the Gaither videos often are, nothing could match the depth of emotion felt that day. I cherish the photographs my wife took during this performance, some of which appear in this book.

If I did not know it before, traveling with James and Mim during these performances showed me what a trouper he really is. To those who have followed James' career closely, it is no secret that he has had some health problems during recent years. He has suffered one major stroke and another minor one, he has had some problems with laryngitis, and his hearing is not as good as he would like. Almost anyone his age (77) could say the same.

Ellistine Holly, James, and Allen performing in Mississippi Chautauqua 1994-1995 at the Old Capitol House Chamber in Jackson, Mississippi.

James' standards for himself are so high that I don't think he was really satisfied with any of his Chautauqua performances. He sometimes felt nauseous, and I think the emotions summoned forth by portraying his beloved nephew often contributed to that. Yet, on every occasion, James was a true professional. No audience ever detected that he was feeling poorly, and years seemed to drop off him whenever he took the stage. I believe that James understood from the first that this was his way of paying tribute to R. W., and he went forward no matter how he felt. When he occasionally mused about "not being himself" at a performance, I reminded him that "50% of James Blackwood's best is better than 100% of almost anyone else."

After the Chautauqua presentations were over, the historian in me demanded that I attempt to do some type of book on James Blackwood. While driving to my parents' home in Athens in September, 1995, I developed the idea which grew into this book, and James graciously allowed me to do so. I thank him for that and for his cooperation. It has truly been a joy and a personal privilege to be in contact with so many of my heroes from gospel and country music who have so generously contributed to this tribute to James. I think it would be safe to say that there has never been a more universally-beloved man than James Blackwood. His fans and fans of those who have contributed to this book will be delighted, amused, touched, and moved by these tributes and stories. Everyone who has contributed to this book has known James far longer than I have, but my respect and admiration for him is second to none. On James' behalf as well as mine, I am sincerely grateful to all who have helped us assemble this tribute to the greatest lead singer and probably the most well-known individual in the history of Southern gospel music.

Brenda and I cherish our friendship with James and Mim, and we are honored that they have taken us into their lives and shared themselves with us. Anywhere the four of us have been together, there has never been a time when someone didn't tentatively walk up to James and say "Aren't you James Blackwood?" James has never failed to be gracious to these people, treating each one as if he or she was the most important fan James ever had.

All of us who are fans of Southern gospel music are well aware that not everyone who sings about Jesus is truly a follower of Jesus. But I and all those who have contributed to this book, as well as millions around the world, can attest that James Blackwood not only talks the talk, but he walks

*James portraying R. W. Blackwood in Mississippi
Chautauqua 1994-1995 at the Old Capitol House Chamber
in Jackson, Mississippi.*

the walk. He loves the Lord with all his heart, and keeps pushing himself even at his age to continue singing simply because he has a burning desire to minister and serve in this way.

I often tease James about his "retiring," which he has already done several times. He "retired" from The Blackwood Brothers in the early 1980s; he "retired" from The Masters V in the late 1980s; he "retired" as a solo artist about 1990; and he claims that he has "retired" from The James Blackwood Quartet in 1996. Yet, even as I write this in July, 1996, he is doing solo dates in New England.

Frankly, I don't believe that James Blackwood will ever retire from singing the music that he loves and the ministry to which God has so obviously called him. As long as there are people who want to hear him sing—which will be always —he will be there as long as airplanes fly or his car will run. One can retire from a profession, but not from a calling.

I devoutly hope that James Blackwood will continue to sing for many more years. I also hope that James is on stage singing when God calls him to come home. Since I know that God has a great sense of timing, I'm certain that is what will happen.

James, thank you for being my friend. Thank you for showing me such a shining example of character, integrity, and absolute class. Most of all, thank you for the songs you have sung which have taught me more about Jesus.

I'll meet you in the Morning.

Allen Dennis
Delta State University

James Blackwood
Memories
by
Some of His Best Friends

John Ashcroft

United States Senator John Ashcroft (R-MO) has had a long and distinguished career in Missouri and national politics. In addition to serving in the Senate, Senator Ashcroft has also served as State Auditor,
Attorney General, and Governor of Missouri. He first met James in
Springfield, Missouri, many years ago. Senator Ashcroft still continues
his musical career as baritone with The Singing Senators, a quartet
composed of four Republican senators, whose appearances include singing *Elvira* at the 1996 Republican National Convention.

My earliest memories of gospel music carry the clarion
crystal voice of James Blackwood. Later in life, when I was
privileged to sing with James and The Masters V, it was as if
I had joined an angel choir.

I am grate-
ful for his strong
Christian testi-
mony and his
warm friendship
to me.

*John
Ashcroft*

Chet Atkins

Chet Atkins is to the guitar what James Blackwood is to gospel music: synonymous. Without question, Chet has set a standard for country guitarists that will never be surpassed. He is "Mr. Guitar," and it only takes a few notes for a seasoned country music fan to recognize the classic Atkins style. Early in James' recording career, Chet produced many of The Blackwood Brothers' earliest recordings, and played guitar on many of them. He is the world's greatest guitarist, recording executive extraordinaire, a country music legend, and a member of the Country Music Hall of Fame.

Sometime during the early 1950s, The Blackwood Brothers were coming to Nashville from Memphis for a recording session. I was the producer, and they were late. When they finally arrived, I could tell that they were all a little upset at Jackie Marshall, their pianist.

They finally told me that they had been stopped by the Highway Patrol for doing 80 miles an hour. James was driving and was very kind and congenial to the officer, who was about to let James off with a warning. Just about the time that the officer was going to let them go, Jackie spoke up from the back seat, "I'm going to pray for you, officer." When the officer inquired why, Jackie said "For lying. We were only doing 70."

Much to James' disgust, the patrolman then issued him a ticket. We worked in that recording session for three or four hours, and Jackie took a lot of serious ribbing from everyone.

Les Beasley

A native of Louisiana, Les Beasley has sung lead with The Florida Boys
for more than forty years, and is a long-time resident of Pensacola.
Although tenors in the quartet may come and go, Les, Glen Allred
(baritone), Derrell Stewart (piano), and Buddy Liles (bass) have made
The Florida Boys one of the nation's best-known and most beloved
gospel quartets. Les served as the third President of the Gospel Music
Association, and James calls him "the ideal quartet manager."

Many years ago, James and I were on a Greek ship in
the Mediterranean Sea in cabins across from one another.

Les Beasley

We were en route from Athens, Greece, to Beirut, Lebanon.

It had been a tiring trip. We had flown from Nashville to Bangor, Maine, and then on to Athens. We toured Athens and Corinth all day, and when we returned to our ship, I immediately went to bed.

About 2:30 or 3:00 the next morning, I got up, awakened my wife, and asked her if she would like to go walking on the deck. I have forgotten exactly what she said, but it amounted to "no." However, almost as soon as I had left, she decided to get up, get dressed, and join me. Then she discovered that I had locked her inside our cabin and had taken the key.

Then she started beating on the door until she awakened James across in the next cabin and got him to come to the door. She asked James to go look for me, and James graciously honored her request, although he didn't find me.

I'm not sure that James has ever forgiven me for that. I know my wife hasn't.

Dan Betzer

James became acquainted with Dan Betzer, a native of Sioux City, Iowa, during The Blackwoods' stay in Shenandoah. Dan was a student in an early music school operated by The Blackwoods in Shenandoah. An Assembly of God minister, Dan has been the featured speaker on the "Revival Time" broadcast, the international broadcast of the Assemblies of God, for more than twenty years. He is currently the pastor of the First Assembly of God in Fort Myers, Florida.

My friendship with the legendary James Blackwood goes back to the mid-1940s. My family lived in Sioux City, Iowa, home of the stockyards along the Mississippi River. My father was a barber who loved music—especially The Blackwood Brothers. My dad had two heroes in life at that time: the Apostle Paul and James Blackwood. The Blackwood Brothers quartet was headquartered at that time in Shenandoah, Iowa, about 175 miles south of Sioux City. Anytime the group gave a concert within a hundred miles or so of our home, the Betzer family was present, usually on the front row.

At the time of my story, the quartet consisted of Cat Freeman (brother of Vestal Goodman), tenor; James Blackwood, lead; R.W. Blackwood, baritone; Bill Lyles, bass; and Hilton Griswold at the piano. The Blackwoods were coming to give a concert in Sioux City, and my dad contacted them to ask if they would be our guests for dinner just before the concert. To our delight, they agreed to come.

We were not well-to-do, and our home was tiny. However, mom and dad were determined to give the quartet the royal treatment. Mom called in some of my relatives and cooked all day to prepare something unusual. It was a concoction that featured chicken. It was very good, as I recall, but it *looked* strange; almost exotic.

Early that afternoon, in their live broadcast from KMA in Shenandoah, James promoted the concert that night in Sioux City and informed the listeners that the quartet was coming to our home for dinner. As was their custom, the quartet would croon into the microphone "Hmmmmmm-mmmmmmmm," indicating that their hunger would be at its zenith. How thrilled we were to hear on the radio that the world's greatest quartet would be our guests that very day. And throughout the afternoon, the aroma of that chicken concoction filled the house.

At the appointed time, The Blackwoods' big Chrysler pulled in front of our home, and Dad welcomed the famous singers into the living room. I can still remember Hilton sitting down at our old upright piano, playing some tune in that inimitable Griswold style.

Mom had set the table so that I could sit between James and R.W. Wow! That was some thrill to a little boy's heart! The food was placed on the table, Dad said grace, and we began to eat. There were vegetables, breads, mashed potatoes, salad, and that strange chicken dish.

I watched R.W. tear into it, with those trademark eyebrows rising, as he tried to figure out what he was eating. Mom had put everything she had into that chicken, trying to stretch it as far as possible.

The quartet was very kind, saying all the right words and making Mom feel that she was an early version of Julia Child. They sang a little song for us, thanked everyone, and left for the concert. Oh, the feeling in our home! The Blackwood Brothers had been there! We quickly cleaned up the dishes and made our way to the concert. It was wonderful, as always, with R.W. fanning Hilton's hands as he played something fast, with Bill Lyles feigning terror as he had to sing a tenor part, with Cat Freeman hitting notes so high that I don't think they are even on a piano, and with James leading the way with his classy remarks. After the concert, we bought the records we didn't already have and drove home in silence. It was a day we would never forget!

The next morning, we tuned in to KMA for The Blackwood Brothers' first radio show of the day. We wondered, "Would they mention being at our house the night before?" Yes, they did! They actually spoke our name on the radio! And R.W. said how much he enjoyed the dinner. Then he said to James, "I never ate anything like Mrs. Betzer fixed last night. What do you think it was?" After a short silence, James responded, "Well . . . it was chicken, I guess."

In later years, every time Mom fixed that particular dish, we would laugh and say, "Here comes the chicken-I-guess."

Billy Blackwood

Billy Blackwood is the younger son of James and Mim. He played drums with The Blackwood Brothers Quartet for a time, and later played with Voice, an opening act for Elvis Presley. He is an accomplished singer, musician, and songwriter, and serves as a minister with the Hendersonville Chapel, an interdenominational church in Hendersonville, Tennessee. His main focus is the Praise and Worship ministry and visitation.

M y story has to do with the speed and aggressiveness with which my dad approaches everything in life; in this instance, it was a T-shirt. I was about 12 or 13 and happened to be in my parents' room while my dad was getting

Billy Blackwood

dressed. My mom was also there, and I think we were probably getting ready to run an errand or go to the store.

Somehow, my undershirts had gotten mixed in with dad's in his undershirt drawer. It must be understood that my dad has only two speeds: off and attack. If he prepares to do something, he goes after it with lightning speed and fierce determination, not maliciously, but with total commitment.

This particular morning, his object was a T-shirt. Watching him put on a T-shirt was always comical, but this was a particularly hilarious attempt as he reached in his drawer, mistakenly grabbed one of my T-shirts, and wrestled it on. It was like watching a madman trying to get out of a straitjacket; or, in this case, trying to get into one!

If there were ever an Olympic event for getting dressed, he would win the gold medal every time. His speed is unequaled! Yet this morning there was a sudden pause in the routine as he conquered that shirt, only to realize that it was several sizes too small. My mom and I almost needed oxygen as we went into convulsive laughter at seeing my dad look down in wonder and the T-shirt/girdle he had miraculously managed to squeeze into.

As my mom and I gasped for breath, he nearly did us in by remarking "I believe this T-shirt is too small!" To this day, this story comes up whenever we reminisce about funny family times. My dad is the most unintentionally funny man who ever lived.

On a more serious note, I want to share the most important thing my dad has taught me, and it's the most important thing any parent can teach a child. The greatest asset in life isn't houses or land, social standing, education, or being widely traveled. The greatest asset in life is an accurate understanding of God's love for us. In possession of that knowledge, we can face any crisis or circumstance and come through victorious. God's love is the sustaining force of life.

A parent's greatest responsibility is to mirror that love and to exemplify it to the best of his or her ability. In that, my father and mother have excelled. I have never doubted their love for me. Even during my rebellious teenage years, my parents, though expressing their concern and disappointment, never failed to couch those feelings in steadfast love.

The following verse says it better than I can. I saw it on the back of a Hallmark card many years ago. It is a tribute to the two most wonderful people I know.

I could never repay what you taught when I was small
Or give to you both gift for gift the daily treasures I recall
But there's one gift I can give; it's all the love you've earned
For love is what you always taught and love is what I learned.

Cecil Blackwood

Cecil Blackwood, one of James' nephews, is the younger brother of the legendary baritone R.W. Blackwood. At the time of R.W.'s death, Cecil was 19 years of age and was singing in a group called The Songfellows Quartet. Within a few weeks, Cecil began singing the baritone part in The Blackwood Brothers Quartet, and continues to do so today. In the 63-year history of The Blackwood Brothers Quartet, R.W. and Cecil have been the group's only full-time baritones. Cecil is a resident of Germantown, Tennessee, and continues to tour with The Blackwood Brothers.

I have known James Blackwood longer than any other living person. I can remember James having the chicken pox when I was about two years old, and that he came to visit me and my family. Within about two weeks, I had the chicken pox, and I can still recall the itching and the scratching. So I can say that I caught the chicken pox from James Blackwood.

After the quartet moved to Jackson, Mississippi, I can remember that it was a big treat for me to go across the street from the hotel where we lived to eat a 5-cent Krystal hamburger with James and R.W. We then moved with the quartet to Shreveport and then to Shenandoah, Iowa, where I started kindergarten. I can remember sitting on the front row watching The Blackwood Brothers in concert, and particularly watching James. James was very skinny in those days, and had a great deal of vibrato to his voice. Consequently, his Adam's apple would fly up and down with his vibrato, and that always kept my attention.

I can remember James telling me how he had his schedule timed just right so that he could get all the sleep he could before he went to the radio station in Shenandoah

Cecil and James with The Mandrell Sisters (Irlene, Louise, and Barbara) during a television taping about 1980.

for The Blackwood Brothers' morning radio program. Many times the group had been several hundred miles away the night before doing a concert, and got back home in the wee hours of the morning. So James had it timed so that he often walked in the door at KMA just as Hilton gave the roll on *Give the World a Smile,* and James would be there just in time to join in.

In 1950, we all moved to Memphis and settled in the same general area of east Memphis. We attended the First Assembly of God church, where I and several other young men about my age formed a group we called The Songfellows Quartet. I can well remember that a young man named Elvis Presley used to practice with us and ride around in the car with us. The Songfellows had gotten good enough to open for The Blackwood Brothers at the Ellis Auditorium, and I think that James and R.W. had begun to recognize that we had a pretty good group.

After R.W. was killed on June 30, 1954, I was the logical choice to replace him in The Blackwood Brothers Quartet, since I was already singing baritone and knew all of his songs. My first concert with The Blackwood Brothers was in Little Rock, Arkansas, where James Wetherington, the "Big Chief" of The Statesmen Quartet, sang bass, along with James on lead, Bill Shaw on tenor, and Jackie Marshall at the piano. J.D. Sumner then joined us on bass in a concert at Clanton, Alabama, where R.W. and Bill had been killed, marking the first appearance of the reconstituted quartet.

I looked to James not only as the quartet leader, but also as the leader of our family and our spiritual leader. At first, James did everything. He drove the car, booked the concerts, did the emceeing, and sang the lead. He carried the full load of the group almost by himself. After a little while, we realized that James could not continue to do all these things by himself, so we sat down and designated the different jobs that we should each have. J.D. was assigned to the public address system, I was assigned to the record table, Bill Shaw was to help me, and Jackie Marshall was to help J.D. We also began to share the driving.

James was constantly looking for new songs for the quartet to sing. He was especially interested in gospel songs that might have been recorded by secular artists. He would bring new songs to the group, and we would all share ideas about arrangements. The Blackwood Brothers appeared on the Arthur Godfrey Talent Scouts a second time, and won again. I remember seeing the applause meter hit the peg at the far right end of it, and I jumped up, saying "We won, we won!" James said "Shhh! Sit down, it hasn't been announced yet."

After we acquired our first bus, we were traveling in either Michigan or Ohio one day, and James was taking a turn at the wheel. Usually J.D. or I would drive the bus, but this day James was driving. The brakes on our bus weren't too good, particularly when they got wet. This day was snowy and wet, and James drove right past a toll booth at about sixty miles an hour, unable to stop. "I have no brakes, I have no brakes!" said James, standing straight up on the brake pedal while holding onto the steering wheel with both hands. Finally, about a quarter of a mile past the toll booth, James brought the bus to a stop, put it in reverse, backed up to the toll booth, paid the toll, and went on as if nothing had happened.

I remember our singing one night in New England at a Baptist church which had a rounded stage with a little separate section in front for the pulpit. Well, they took the pulpit section away for our concert, leaving the stage not perfectly round. We were doing a song called *Mail Order From Heaven*, and there's a line in the song that says "Fall down on your knees," and James went down on his knees, but there was no stage where James' right knee went. He turned a complete somersault, landed on his feet, microphone still in hand, and continued singing as if nothing had happened. But the other three of us had to leave the stage roaring in laughter. (James was upset at us for laughing and told us to get off the stage.)

At least two or three times a year, James would call us together and remind us that he knew we weren't perfect, but that he expected us to act in a way that would uphold the name of The Blackwood Brothers, and to live the life that we sang about. I've always been glad that we had a James Blackwood to lead our group in that way, because some groups didn't have that kind of leadership.

I also think that James deserves some credit for helping J.D. Sumner become a great gospel songwriter. James would give J.D. an idea or a line for a song, and J.D. would get his guitar out and before very long have a song written based on what James had said. James was also my inspiration as an emcee, for I began to take on more of that role after James stepped down as a full-time member of the quartet. I tried to pattern my style after James, and he would give me advice.

James could always sing all four parts in the quartet, and could help anyone else in the group hit the right note when we were practicing. He helped us learn more than just our own part, so that we understood better how all the parts were supposed to blend together. James also always encouraged me in various business ventures, giving me advice and green lights and "go-ahead" signals as we established several businesses.

I believe James Blackwood to really be the King of Gospel Music, and is someone people can look up to as a respectable gospel singer who lives the life he sings about. He is respected by everyone involved in gospel music; singers, manufacturers, deejays, and many others have always looked up to James Blackwood as the patriarch of gospel music. He is not only the leader of our family, but is the leading figure in gospel music. He is respected not only by gospel singers, but by country and pop singers as well.

James will go down in history as a pioneer, a leader, a principled and honest businessman, and someone other singers can look up to as a father image and a leader image, and as someone they can attempt to shape their lives by. I give James the credit for anything that I might have achieved in the music business during these last forty-two years. He has not only guided me, but hundreds of other gospel singers as well.

Although James Blackwood is short in stature, he will go down in history head and shoulders above all other gospel singers.

Jimmy Blackwood

Jimmy Blackwood, the elder son of James and Mim, first sang in an organized quartet with The Junior Blackwood Brothers, beginning in the early 1960s. He later sang lead with The Stamps Quartet, and joined The Blackwood Brothers as lead singer in 1971 when James elected to scale back his role with the quartet. Jimmy remained with The Blackwood Brothers until 1984, when he began a highly successful solo ministry which continues today. Although he no longer sings full-time in a quartet, Jimmy unquestionably has one of the purest lead voices in gospel music.

Just mention the name of James Blackwood, and people all around the world have their own way of showing respect. All recognize his God-given talent and admire his faithfulness in singing the gospel for over sixty years. He is regarded as "Mr. Gospel Music" by his peers. His fans respectfully call him "Mr. Blackwood," and his friends just call him James. He named me after himself, and I get to call him Daddy.

There is a special blessing in being the son of a man who is admired by so many people, and there has always been a special relationship between us. Once when I was very young, Daddy went somewhere to sing and I tried to follow him on my tricycle. Mama found me several blocks away from home, pedaling away. I was about five years old before I realized that my playmates' fathers didn't sing in gospel quartets.

One year I got a toy spinner for Christmas. I was so young that I didn't know it wouldn't spin on top of Daddy's head. I don't remember how long it took to get that thing out of his hair! I found a top similar to that one a few years ago and gave it to him as a Christmas present. He probably

Jimmy Blackwood

didn't think the experience with the first top was very funny at the time, but we all laugh about it now.

Although he raised me with firm discipline, I never once doubted his love for me. In fact, it was because of his love for me that he would apply "firm conviction to the seat of correction" to keep my life headed in the right direction.

He established a high standard of excellence for me to follow, and I am blessed to be able to walk in his shadow and follow in his footsteps. I remember one night when I was singing lead in the quartet that he came to me after the concert and said "You did a good job, son." I knew he wouldn't hand out compliments if he didn't mean them. That statement meant a great deal to me, because it showed that I not only had his love, but that I also had his approval as a singer.

Another episode in our lives illustrates the kind of love and special relationship we have. In 1984, I was singing lead with The Blackwood Brothers and Daddy was singing with The Masters V. In March of that year, I was admitted to the hospital in Memphis, and was diagnosed with cancer of the pancreas. The Masters V were singing at a church in Spokane, Washington, when word reached them that I had cancer and that the doctors didn't know if I could survive an operation. Daddy threw his arms up toward heaven and cried "Oh, Lord, just take me and leave my son!" He flew all night and most of the next day to get to the hospital to be with me. No doubt he prayed all the way home. God honored his prayers and those of many others, for which I am so thankful.

I have a full life with a wonderful wife, beautiful children and grandchildren, and a rewarding ministry. I owe my Daddy a debt of gratitude and a debt of love, for I am welcomed into churches and the hearts of people today because of the integrity of my Daddy's life and ministry. Recently, a man came to one of my services to tell me that my Daddy had led him to the Lord more than forty years ago. His entire family had become Christians because of Daddy.

How can one best measure the life of this man? Some

might point to his rise from the obscurity of a Mississippi sharecropper's farm to a place of world-wide recognition, while others might point to his Grammy awards or Dove awards. As the elder son of a man who has more friends than he can count, I must simply say "He pointed me to Jesus." I love you, Daddy.

It is often said that behind every great man there is a great woman, and that is certainly true in this case. These reflections on my Daddy's life would not be complete without recognizing the important role played by my Mother in supporting Daddy and in rearing me and my brother Billy. None of us would be where we are today if it had not been for the love, patience, and support of this very special lady. I love you too, Mama.

Mim Blackwood

Miriam (Mim) Grantham Blackwood is a native of Weathersby, Mississippi, and married James on May 4, 1939. She and James have two sons, four grandchildren, and four great-grandchildren. According to James, everyone who has ever sung or played piano with The Blackwood Brothers sooner or later always made the comment that Mim was the perfect wife for a traveling quartet member. James says that Mim is the perfect wife, period.

In the 1950s, James won an award that named him "Mr. Gospel Music." Jimmy, Billy, and I sent him a telegram that read "Congratulations to the one who is Mr. Everything to us." We still feel the same way.

I am very grateful that God has allowed me to have fifty-seven years with the man I fell in love with and married when I was seventeen years old. Given the same opportunity, I would do it all over again.

Mim and James at a Grammy awards banquet in the mid-1970s.

41

God has blessed us with a wonderful family and a host of friends as a result of James' gospel singing ministry. I am glad he has used his God-given talent to sing gospel songs that have been a blessing to people all over the world. I think James has the most beautiful voice I have ever heard.

I have often been asked how I coped with James' being away from home so much, and I have borrowed an answer from Mrs. Billy (Ruth) Graham. She answered the same question about her husband by saying she had rather be with Billy part of the time than with anyone else all of the time. I knew I felt that way about James, but didn't know how to express it as well as she.

I can sum up my feelings about our life together in just a few words: I am very proud to be Mrs. James Blackwood.

Paul R. Boden

Paul Boden is editor of the *U.S. Gospel News,* a leading newspaper of Southern gospel music. He is headquartered in Jonesboro, Arkansas, where he also owns and operates radio station KNEA, a leading gospel music station. Paul has been an effective promoter and supporter of gospel music for many years.

James Blackwood, his life, his family, his talent and his influence have touched millions of people. I consider it a great honor to be known as one of his friends.

In recalling the years I've known James and observed his accomplishments, a flood of events come to mind. I remember visits to The Blackwood Brothers record shop in downtown Memphis; I remember the National Quartet Convention, which was held for many years at the Ellis Auditorium on the banks of the Mississippi, and which James and the quartet so ably hosted. I also remember the time The Blackwood Brothers won the Arthur Godfrey Talent Scouts competition, and how proud they made all of us who love gospel music.

But there is one event that stands out in my mind when I think of James. Joe Kelsey and The Songmasters (from Milan, Tennessee) were scheduled to sing on one of Lloyd Orrell's great all-night concerts in Indianapolis, Indiana. Joe invited me to ride up on the bus and enjoy the weekend. Many famous groups and artists were scheduled to appear: The Kingsmen, The Couriers, Jerry and The Goffs, The Sego Brothers and Naomi, The Blackwood Brothers, and others. It was one of those nights when every group just outdid themselves.

During The Blackwood Brothers' portion of the concert, James stepped to the microphone and read a letter he had just written to Anita Bryant, an outspoken opponent of the homosexual lifestyle. She had really been under fire from the media and others about this issue. James left no doubt in anyone's mind where he stood on this issue.

When he finished reading the letter, the sold-out crowd stood and applauded to show their approval of James' letter. The Blackwood Brothers began to sing as the crowd was experiencing "near rapture" status. James jumped from the stage, which was located at home plate of Indian Stadium, and proceeded to run the bases while the rest of the group continued to sing.

After circling the bases, James jumped back onstage, grabbed the microphone again without a hint of showing the effects of his "Run for Jesus," and launched into his trademark song *I'll Meet You in the Morning.* I've attended gospel concerts for many years, but that evening in Indianapolis was one I'll never forget.

For some time, I've planned on doing a feature in *U.S. Gospel News* honoring the Greatest of the Greats in gospel music. When I get around to doing this, I know who I'll begin with—Dr. James Blackwood.

Paul R. Boden

44

Bob Brumley

Bob Brumley is the son of Albert E. Brumley, one of the most famous gospel songwriters of all time. Bob is actively engaged with the Albert E. Brumley and Sons Publishing Company, and also with the Hartford Publishing Company. He lives now in Powell, Missouri, and annually hosts the Albert E. Brumley "Sing" in Springdale, Arkansas.

I have known James Blackwood for more than 40 years. He was a very close friend of my father's, and often visited in his home in Powell, Missouri. I have many memories about James, but one stands out above all the others.

In August, 1971, we booked The Blackwood Brothers as one of the groups appearing at our Third Annual Sundown to Sunup Gospel Sing in Springdale, Arkansas. The event is held outside in a rodeo arena, and at that time we were only having a one-night program. Rain is always a threat for an open-air performance, and at mid-afternoon dark clouds began to gather. My brother Bill and I began to worry as the skies darkened, but when rain began we came close to panic. We had thousands of people waiting to be entertained, many from out of state, and we did not want them to be disappointed.

After a frantic discussion, it was decided to use the high school auditorium for the concert. At six o'clock, we opened the doors and in a very short time the seats were all filled, with long lines of people still waiting to get in. But there was no place to put them. In the meantime, the rain had stopped and it was turning into a pretty nice evening. It was still pretty wet, but we decided to go back to the rodeo arena with the remaining ticket holders and have two concerts going at the same time.

I must say that the quartets and other singing groups

Bob Brumley

were very cooperative. When each finished at one location, we bussed them across town to the other. The rodeo arena was ankle-deep in mud, the bleachers were damp, and there were naturally some delays. But no one complained. When it came time for The Blackwood Brothers to sing at the arena, I think James must have been wondering what he was going to do when the quartet sang *I'll Meet You In the Morning*.

As anyone knows who has watched James and The Blackwoods perform, it was traditional for James to come down from the stage and mingle with the crowd while singing this song. But this time the floor of the arena was a sea of mud and no seating had been set up because of this. James, being the consummate performer that he is, was not going to let a little mud deter him. When it came time to do *I'll Meet You In the Morning*, he simply took off his shoes and socks, rolled up his pants legs, and came off the stage. He stood and walked in the mud to sing to his audience as he always did.

The crowd came to its feet and stood for the entire song, and James gave the performance of his life. The Oak Ridge Boys were scheduled to appear right after The Blackwoods, and their lead singer Duane Allen turned to me and said "There ain't no way we can follow that!" It was truly an awe-inspiring time for the Brumley Sing, and is an event that is still talked about 25 years later.

James has always been an inspiration to me and to others. He has always been willing to go the extra mile to help in any way he can, and I will always be thankful to him for the many times and many ways he has helped me in my efforts. I love him and I thank him for being my friend and brother.

Wouldn't it be wonderful if we could keep James singing for another sixty-three years?

Johnny Cash

Johnny Cash is on everyone's short list of genuine country music legends. As singer, songwriter, concert artist, TV personality, and social critic, Johnny has few if any peers. He began his recording career with Sun Records in 1955, and has also recorded with Columbia and Mercury. His long list of hits which have become American classics include *I Walk the Line, Ring of Fire, A Boy Named Sue,* and *Daddy Sang Bass.* He is a member of the Country Music Hall of Fame.

When I was a boy growing up in Dyess, Arkansas, I remember coming in from the fields many times to listen to The Blackwood Brothers Quartet. It never occurred to me that James Blackwood would become my friend, and it cer-

Johnny with James and Dr. Billy Graham at a taping of The Johnny Cash Show in the early 1970s.

tainly never occurred to me that he would later record a
gospel song I had written entitled *Over the Next Hill We'll
Be Home.* That is certainly one of the biggest thrills and
honors I have ever had.

When James was a guest on my ABC television show in
1970, it was one of the biggest thrills of my life. I told him,
"I've always wanted to be a gospel singer like you." James
said, "You are a gospel singer, but not like me. You have a
great ministry of your own."

I've always appreciated that comment from James. He's
a good man, and I'm proud to call him my friend.

Jimmie Davis

Governor Jimmie Davis of Louisiana holds many titles in the fields of country and gospel music: pioneer, singer, songwriter, and distinguished elder statesman. Now in his mid-90s, Governor Davis continues to perform occasionally, appearing on the Grand Ole Opry as recently as 1996. He is a member of the Country Music Hall of Fame, and is the author of many gospel and country songs, including *Someone To Care* and the perennial favorite *You Are My Sunshine.* At James' request, he served as the second President of the Gospel Music Association. He lives in Shreveport.

I am certainly sorry that James Blackwood has decided to give up touring and singing gospel music full time. Perhaps, after sixty-three years, we can allow that! I know he

Jimmie Davis

will still enjoy his occasional dates throughout the country and I know that the people will always enjoy hearing him.

I remember so well when he and the other members of the quartet operated out of Shreveport, Louisiana, and how well they were received in that part of the state. I think his was the first gospel group that performed in Shreveport for any length of time.

James is a great person with a great personality. I often refer to him as a good "salesman" also. He knows what people want and what they don't want, and he knows how to give them what they want when it comes to good gospel entertainment.

I will always be wishing him and his family the best of the Lord's blessings.

Ann Downing

Ann, one of James' fellow Mississippians, sang with The Speer Family early in her career, and later spent many years with her family's group, The Downings. A Dove Award winner for Best Female Vocalist, Ann in recent years has had a very successful solo ministry, concentrating on workshops. She has certainly one of the finest voices in Southern gospel music.

My favorite memory of James Blackwood is also one of the funniest things I have ever seen in my life. Sometime during the early 1970s, The Blackwood Brothers, The Thrasher Brothers, and The Downings were touring the

Ann Downing

Holy Land and adjacent areas. Although the entire trip was wonderful, there is one special memory involving James. I even have a picture of it, if I could just lay my hands on it.

We were in the area of Caesarea, touring the ruins of a gymnasium. Our tour guide was very graphic, pointing out various aspects of the gymnasium which seem archaic today but then were far ahead of their time. In these ruins were the remains of an ancient toilet, consisting of a long concrete slab with holes cut in it, underneath which a stream of water had flowed to cleanse the facility.

While James was listening to the tour guide, he simply took a seat on this concrete slab. My husband Paul quickly grabbed his camera and took a picture of the event, which has brought us many laughs through the years.

I could tell many more serious stories about James, for we are from the same state (Mississippi), and have shared so much in our personal lives and in our careers. I have talked with James enough to know that he agrees that our upbringing and our careers have been a great blessing to us.

But I can never forget that funny event in those ancient ruins so many years ago!

Phil Enloe

Phil Enloe sings baritone with The Couriers, a noted gospel trio which also contains Phil's brother Neil on lead and Duane Nicholson on tenor. Phil sang bass with The Junior Blackwoods many years ago, and had an effective solo ministry between his stints with The Junior Blackwoods and The Couriers. Phil is one of the few gospel singers who can handle both the baritone and bass parts effectively.

As long as I can remember, James Blackwood and the famous Blackwood Brothers Quartet have been the premiere gospel singers. James Blackwood pioneered the style and approach that almost every gospel singer has tried to emulate. He forged an industry which not only helped the church, but also cultivated a pure art form. Long before people began to categorize gospel music styles, James Blackwood begat it all.

Prior to the explosive success of The Blackwood Brothers, no one had ever heard music quite like theirs. They were quickly signed to a recording contract with RCA, appeared often on national television, and sold so many records that music store owners created religious music sections. James' vision of singing the Gospel around the world came to fruition early in his career and has skyrocketed beyond even his own wildest dreams. Because of his integrity and amazing success, the way was paved for countless others to follow, and I am only one of many who have followed the trail which he blazed.

In 1962, James and The Blackwood Brothers Quartet decided to purchase a new motor coach, which would be the quartet's third bus. This mode of transportation revo-

Phil Enloe

lutionized the way gospel, country, and rock groups traveled, and J.D. Sumner, I believe, came up with the idea. The Blackwoods' first two buses were truly Greyhound rejects, and taxed the group's financial resources to pay the daily repair bills!

After squeezing the last bit of life out of their second bus, J.D. put it up for sale. He found a buyer, and sold the old 1948 GMC Silversides Coach to a newly-formed quartet from Portland, Oregon, called The Marks Quartet. But by the time this group acquired the vehicle, it was longing for eternal rest. When I joined the quartet a year later, they had already been brought to the brink of financial ruin by daily resuscitating this weary hunk of metal.

Dean Brown, of Memphis, had preceded my arrival in the group by only two months. The day I arrived, Dean was given the job of orienting me with all the operations, chores, and activities of The Marks. His first and most important task was to give me a tour of THE BUS, my new home. "This bus," said Dean, "is the ACTUAL bus which belonged to none other than the famous Blackwood Brothers Quartet, and they used it for several years." "Wow," I said, "you're kidding!" Then Dean pointed out the faint outline of "Blackwood Brothers" which still remained on the side of the bus. "Soon," Dean boasted, "new paint will cover all of this with our name, 'The Marks'."

Stepping up into the open door, Dean continued. "You are about to step into the Air Force One of gospel music!" When I climbed aboard, the feeling I experienced was difficult to describe. Although I had never met James, the aura of his presence seemed to linger in that old coach. I could almost see Bill Shaw, Cecil Blackwood, J.D. Sumner, Wally Varner, Jackie Marshall, Bundy Brewster (the driver), and Mr. Gospel Music himself, James Blackwood. They had probably spent more time on this bus than they had in their individual homes, and echoes of their music still reverberated. It should have been in a museum, yet we were privileged to own it.

"This was once Bill Shaw's bunk," Dean announced, "and over there is Cecil Blackwood's and there is Wally Varner's." Pointing to another, he said "And this, my good man, is your bunk now. It was once used by the greatest bass singer in the history of the world, J.D. Sumner." I was awestruck. "Go ahead," said Dean, "lie down and try it out. It's your bunk now." "Where is your bunk?" I asked. Dean's eyebrows slowly raised and a big smirk spread across his face as he proclaimed "Right here, pal. I occupy the first class deluxe accommodations of none other than Mr. James Blackwood himself." He gingerly climbed into the bunk, folded his arms respectfully, looked up at a framed picture of James and sighed, "It doesn't get any better than this." We were both wallowing in the limitless potential of our future.

After the rest of the group boarded the bus, we headed out of town for our first engagement. But reality lurked just down the road. As wonderful as this relic was, it was way overdue for the Greyhound Graveyard. To be blunt, we fixed, patched, mended, welded, repaired, renewed, re-placed, retreaded, reconditioned, overhauled, towed, jumpstarted, pulled, pushed, and serviced that old jalopy more than it serviced us. It singlehandedly ended our cor-porate careers and forced us to go our separate ways broke! Finally, we laid it to rest in McCook, Nebraska. May it Rust In Pieces!

Tommy Fairchild

Tommy Fairchild played piano for The Oak Ridge Boys until about the time that famous group decided to focus on country music, at which time he joined The Blackwood Brothers as their pianist. Tommy also devised many classic arrangements for the quartet, including the legendary version of *Blessed Assurance* sung by Pat Hoffmaster. For several years, Tommy lived in Eureka Springs, Arkansas, where he was associated with the Passion Play. He now lives in Florida.

I worked with James for many years, so there are many favorite stories and anecdotes I could tell about him. But I really like to remember the lighter side of the greatest lead singer in the history of gospel music.

James could be quite the practical joker when the mood struck him, and it usually struck him when it came to Ken Turner. He and Ken always seemed to have some nonsense going, but he really broke us up one morning at the Hyatt Regency Hotel in Dearborn, Michigan, while we were sitting around waiting our turn in the shower.

It was Ken's turn to take a shower, and, as usual, he put his teeth in a glass on the lavatory just before he disappeared into the shower. James seized the opportunity. Now picture this, as we were on the top floor: Mr. Dignity picked up that glass, walked down that long hallway with glass in hand, waited for the elevator, took the two-minute ride down to the lobby, walked through the lobby, out the door, and to our bus, which was parked at least a quarter of a mile from the hotel.

James hid the glass on the bus, rushed back to the room, grabbed his newspaper, sat down to read, and assumed the world's most innocent look. This all happened during the short time that Ken was in the shower.

When Ken couldn't find his teeth, he was not amused, but the rest of us had a good laugh. Ken finally found his teeth, and he knew immediately who the guilty party was.

Another vivid memory I have of James occurred somewhere in the Midwest on a hot, humid late summer day. We had played a little county fair somewhere in the middle of nowhere. As I remember, we arrived a little late and didn't have the opportunity to clean up before the show, so one can imagine how dirty and awful we all felt after playing an outdoor show in a rodeo arena. Our immediate goal was to find a hotel room with a hot shower so that we could all be presentable for our next show that evening. But a room was nowhere to be found.

Disappointed and miserable, we finally began the drive to the next show. A few miles out of town, we ran into a rainstorm to end all rainstorms. It was a monster, but it gave one of the brethren an idea. "Jimmy, find a side road and stop the bus. We'll get that shower after all," somebody shouted. The bus stopped and out we went, soap in hand, into that rainstorm.

But just as soon as we all got good and soapy, the rain stopped. There we were, covered with rapidly drying soap, laughing to keep from crying, when out of nowhere came the headlights of an approaching car on that apparently deserted road. Never has a quartet boarded a bus as quickly as we did that memorable day. It was not quite the way most fans picture Mr. Gospel Music!

Larry Ford

One of the truly great tenors in gospel music, Larry sang with The Downings and also sang with The Dixie Echoes before joining The James Blackwood Quartet when Rosie Rozell's health declined. Larry is an ordained Assembly of God minister, and has a solo ministry which he continues when not singing with the quartet. Known for his powerful performances of such songs as *I Don't Know About Tomorrow* and *I Will Sing of My Redeemer* on the Gaither videos, Larry is said by James to be the "finest tenor active in gospel music today."

When I think about how James Blackwood looks and how he presents himself, I am reminded of a prince or a duke. He carries himself with such dignity. No matter how long we have been on the road, or how weary he may be, he is always dressed neatly. He is an elegant man. As I sit thinking about him and how he looks, it strikes me that he looks like an ambassador or some important international figure. And then I realize that he *is* an important international figure. The music of The Blackwoods has reached around the world. It has been my privilege to travel with him to Europe and to Russia, and on a recent trip to the United Kingdom, many asked me about his health and ministry. He *is* truly an ambassador—an ambassador for Christ.

After more than sixty years of singing and speaking about the Savior, it is still new and fresh to him. After singing for thirty years myself, I sometimes want to stay on the bus or in the pastor's study, or hide somewhere until the group is ready to sing. It would certainly not be inappropriate for the principal artist in a group, which James certainly is in The James Blackwood Quartet, to stay out of sight and rest as much as possible. It might be wiser for him to not expend energy before a concert by mingling and visiting with the congregation. Often, that is an effort for me. But for James, meeting and welcoming the people who have come to hear him sing is a spontaneous expression of his relationship with them as his brothers and sisters in Christ.

On a three-week tour to the west coast and back, we were at the end of the tour, tired, and headed for home. One of our last concerts was at a large church in Arkansas. About thirty minutes before the service, Ken Turner, Ray Shelton, Brad White, and I started looking for James to ask him something about the order of the service.

Larry Ford and James during a James Blackwood Quartet concert, First Assembly of God, Memphis, Tennessee.

61

We found him in the sanctuary, making his way along the aisles and into the pews, shaking hands, hugging necks, and sharing himself with others. He *loves* people, and I guess that's the reason people love him so much.

The character that people see on the platform when James sings is not a public *persona*. James is gracious, constant, dependable, and a man of his word. He always takes the time to listen to our individual concerns. He often has a gentle word of wisdom to offer and is always encouraging. He is often a peacemaker! Whatever success our quartet has enjoyed in the past six years is because we have all tried to live up to the standards James sets, not only in performing, but in our personal testimonies of who we are in Christ. James is a lighthouse.

To hear how he sings at 77 years of age is an experience. To sing with him as he worships in spirit and in truth is a double blessing. But, having known James for all these years, I realize that it is not just sharing the gift of his talent or his ministry to which people respond. James shares *himself*. He gives of himself everywhere we go, to big cities or small towns; to Washington state or southwest Florida. James loves people, and do they truly love him. *We* love him.

Bill Gaither

Bill Gaither is one of the two or three finest songwriters in the history of Southern gospel music. During the last few years, Bill and his wife Gloria have revolutionized the gospel music industry with their videos featuring their "Homecoming Friends" in the Gaither studios in Alexandria, Indiana, and at other venues around the country. No one has done more in the last two or three decades to revitalize and popularize gospel music than Bill and Gloria Gaither. Among their many famous songs are *It is Finished!*, *Because He Lives*, *He Touched Me*, and *The King is Coming*.

Whenhen I was in the seventh grade, I heard my first Blackwood Brothers record. It was on RCA Victor, and was *I Won't Have to Cross Jordan Alone* on one side with *Rocka My Soul* on the other side. That started my interest in The Blackwood Brothers, and I followed them closely while I was in junior high and high school.

By the time I was nineteen years old, I was in a quartet called The Pathfinders Quartet, and we were the opening act for a Blackwood Brothers-Statesmen concert. The Blackwoods and The Statesmen were already tremendous stars by this time, with several long-play albums. Our little quartet had only recorded one 78 RPM record with *Rain, Rain, Rain* on one side and *Suppertime* on the other.

At intermission, when it was time to sell our products, the manager of our group insisted that I go back to our table and hold up our record to see if anyone wanted to buy it. There were 5,000 people there that night, and they were crowded around The Blackwoods' table and The Statesmen's table, but no one wanted to buy our record. After a little while, James came over to me, put his arm around me, and said "How're you doin', Bill?" I said, "Not very well." I

Bill Gaither

remember that with not *too* fond a recollection!

Another time we were with The Blackwoods at a high school auditorium in Mishawaka, where there were probably 1,000 or 1,500 people. By this time I was singing with my brother and my sister in a trio, and we were a little bit better. We sang and gave our program and even sold a few records. Afterwards, we went out to eat with The Blackwood Brothers at a restaurant and James sat at our table. He encouraged us, told us that we had some real potential, and that we should keep on doing what we were doing. It was very encouraging to me as an aspiring gospel singer, even though I was preparing for another career as an English teacher. I did become an English teacher, and taught English for about eight or nine years before our songwriting began to bring in enough money to support us.

Ten years later, I went to the National Quartet Convention in Memphis, where SESAC was going to give me an award for beginning writers. I went with my Mother, and the hall was sold out. I saw James in the lobby and said "James, do you remember me," and he said, "Yes, I do, Bill." I told him that I couldn't find a ticket for my mother, and he said, "Let me help you." He took me to the box office and got us two tickets in the balcony. Then he said, "Do you know how to get up there?" I said I thought so, but James insisted on taking my Mother and me directly to our seats. I was overwhelmed by his kindness, and that he would spend that amount of time with basically a nobody like me. Later on that evening, he came up again to our seat to ask if the seats were all right.

I often tell people that no one gets to the level of a James Blackwood without being sensitive to people's needs. When people mention James or The Blackwood Brothers to me, I often tell them about that episode when James, at the top of his profession, cared enough about a young man from Indiana and his mother to take that sort of time to show his concern.

I have many warm and pleasant memories of James Blackwood.

Larry Gatlin

Never is there tighter harmony than when Larry Gatlin sings with his brothers Steve and Rudy. For more than twenty years, Larry has been a mainstay in country music, and is as noted a songwriter as he is a singer. With songs such as *Broken Lady, Statues Without Hearts, Houston (Means I'm One Day Closer to You),* and the classic *All the Gold in California*, Larry Gatlin and the Gatlin Brothers provide the best example of sibling harmony active today in country music. Larry, Steve, and Rudy perform regularly at the Gatlin Brothers Theatre in Myrtle Beach, South Carolina.

Where do I start to talk about one of my very first heroes, James Blackwood? Wherever I have gone in the world, I have always taken music with me. My brothers and I have sung for millions of people in various venues around the globe, and James Blackwood and his influence have never been far from me.

James is one of three or four people who have had a significant impact on my career, and I can name them all. In addition to James, there was R.W. Blackwood, whom I miss so much, and for whom I cried for three days when I learned that he and Bill had been killed in that horrible plane crash back in the 1950s. Then, there was Jake Hess, the great lead singer for The Statesmen.

I first heard them sing in 1952 in Abilene, Texas, at a little auditorium called the Fairpark Auditorium. My two brothers, Steve and Rudy, were very small. I guess Steve was about two, Rudy was just an infant, and I was five. My mother and father hired a babysitter for Steve and Rudy, and decided to take me with them to the concert, since keeping three young ones would be too much for any one human being!

I will never forget that night and the music I heard. It wasn't as if I didn't know about God or about Jesus, because I went to Sunday School and was a good little Assembly of God boy. I had always enjoyed church and the things of God, but I had never been as inspired as I was that night. To hear these gentlemen sing, to see the look on their faces, and to feel the fervor, the excitement, and the joy with which they presented the music, was more than I could have ever imagined. That night, James Blackwood became one of my very first heroes, and he has done nothing during the intervening 45 years to make him any less of a hero. On the contrary, I admire him more now than ever.

I haven't been able to see James much during the last few years, and I do wish we had been able to do more things together. I am so very happy that James has agreed to be part of a video that Bill Gaither is putting together in which the Gatlin Brothers pay tribute to some of our heroes, including James, Jake Hess, Hovie Lister, and J.D. Sumner.

James is more than a wonderful singer. He is a wonderful man, a wonderful role model, and a wonderful example to everyone. His music is infectious. When I saw him sing that first time in Abilene in 1952, I knew what I wanted to be; I wanted to be a singer. I wanted to try to move people with music the way he moved me that night.

Every time I have gotten to sing with James Blackwood, it has been a wonderful privilege. We appeared with him in places such as Abilene, Odessa, and Lubbock. Much later, when the brothers and I were guest hosts on national television shows, we were privileged to have James as a guest along with the other members of The Masters V. We also recorded an album for one of the Blackwood companies that Cecil helped us with. So, we have a lot of wonderful memories of James Blackwood.

I thank God for James Blackwood and for his influence on my life and my career. I will pray for him and for his continued good health. I love him, I respect him, I love to hear him sing, and I can't wait to hear him sing again. He truly is my hero.

Larry clowns with James, Cecil, and Ken Turner as he emcees a National Academy of Recording Arts and Sciences Awards Banquet at the Memphis Airport Hilton in 1985.

Jerry Goff

James first met Jerry Goff when Jerry was singing with The Thrasher Brothers, who were based in Birmingham, Alabama. Jerry has a nationwide evangelistic ministry, and he and his wife also do extensive missionary work. Jerry writes a regular column for *The Singing News*, and is one of the more astute observers of trends and styles in Southern gospel music.

I don't guess there is anyone who has been more instrumental in spreading gospel music to the far corners of the world than James Blackwood. I was made acutely aware of this many years ago, I think in 1973. My group, The Singing Goffs, was working dates for Harold Lossing of Toronto, Canada. Mr. Lossing asked me if I was interested in opening up new areas to gospel music, and if so, he had a couple of places that he wanted to try. I agreed, and we planned a trip to the northern areas of Canada. To those of us in Tennessee, Toronto is really "up north," but he wanted us to go about 500 miles north of Toronto.

We had four concerts planned, at Sault St. Marie, Sudbury, North Bay, and Timmins. Since Timmins was the farthest north of the four, we decided to open in Timmins and work our way south. It was a really tough trip. Sometimes we could only go ten or fifteen miles an hour because the roads were so bad. After hours and hours of driving, we arrived in Timmins and checked into a motel for a few hours of rest before the concert.

After we showered and dressed, we headed for the little restaurant adjoining the motel. I thought, "Man, this is going to be something! Getting to sing gospel music with all that harmony and rhythm to people who have never heard it before." I could hardly wait.

We settled into a booth and the waitress brought our menus. It was a truly desolate place. Basically, it was nothing except a pile of rocks in the frozen tundra. I thought to myself, "This place is really a no-man's land. No wonder they've never heard of gospel music."

The waitress returned to take our order. I really don't remember what we ordered, but I do remember what happened. After we told her what we wanted, she asked, "What brings you guys to this area? I can tell from the way you talk that you aren't from around here." I said to her, "We're here for a gospel music concert tonight at the local high school. Have you ever heard of gospel music?" I'll never forget her next words: "Have *you* ever heard of James Blackwood? He was here once and I went to hear his group."

This just proves one thing: Anywhere on planet Earth, if you should think you're the first one to sing gospel music to an audience, you'd better ask if they know James Blackwood.

Ed Gosa

Ed Gosa is a Federal District Judge in the Twenty-fourth Judicial Circuit, located in Vernon, Alabama. A life-long Blackwood Brothers fan, Judge Gosa probably has the finest collection of Blackwood Brothers music and memorabilia in the United States. His archive of Southern gospel music and memorabilia in general is also considered perhaps the best such personal collection in the South. James confirms that Judge Gosa is the only adult other than Elvis Presley who consistently refers to him only as "Mr. Blackwood."

In 1951, when I was 11 years old, my family and I first saw The Blackwood Brothers in concert at the grammar school auditorium in Guin, Alabama. The personnel at that time were Dan Huskey, James Blackwood, R.W. Blackwood, Bill Lyles, with Jackie Marshall at the piano. We saw them again the next year, by which time Bill Shaw had replaced Dan Huskey. R.W. was having throat problems that year, and Doyle Blackwood sang the baritone part.

I never dreamed at that time that one day I would know Mr. Blackwood on a personal basis. I consider him one of the greatest Americans of the twentieth century. I could never address him as "James" without prefacing it with "Brother" or "Doctor." In fact, he once told me that only two people always referred to him as "Mr. Blackwood" - Elvis Presley and I.

Beginning in 1975, I promoted The Blackwood Brothers in concert in Vernon, Alabama, for ten consecutive years. On one occasion, they were to sing in our church on Sunday afternoon after appearing at an all-night singing in Birmingham the night before. On my way to Sunday School, I observed their bus in the school parking lot. While they

Ed Gosa

were setting up their equipment after church, I asked Cecil, Jimmy, Ken, Pat, and Tommy what time they had arrived in Vernon. Jimmy replied that they had arrived about 3:00 a.m., but that his father was not pleased with their performance in Birmingham the night before, and upon their arrival in Vernon he rehearsed them for two hours before they could retire to their bunks on the bus! Incidentally, Mr. Blackwood had been in the 11:00 a.m. church service that morning.

Another memorable occasion came when the quartet was in our church for another Sunday afternoon concert some years later. Mr. Blackwood told me that he was going to perform a new song written by Bill Gaither than had not yet been published. That afternoon, he gave what must have been one of the first public performances of the classic *It Is Finished!*, and had to do an encore. That same day, our pastor Ed Broadway asked Mr. Blackwood if they were going to do *When The Saints Go Marching In*, with Ken Turner doing the horn imitations. Mr. Blackwood replied that they did not normally do that song when they appeared in churches. But at the pastor's request, they performed it, with Ken doing his imitation of Louis Armstrong. It brought the house down, and they never failed to do it every time thereafter when they appeared at our church.

I hesitate to bring up another incident, because it reveals how brazen I was at age 20, but I will tell the story anyway. In 1960, while I was attending the University of North Alabama in Florence, about 20 of us went to nearby Decatur to a Blackwood-Statesmen concert. At the intermission, I wanted to request *Give the World A Smile*, but I was afraid to approach Mr. Blackwood. But I did get up the nerve to talk to Cecil, and he quickly advised me that I would have to ask James. I finally did ask him if they would do the song, but at the conclusion of their performance they had not sung it.

I am embarrassed now to admit that I jumped up from my seat and said "James, you did not do *Give the World A Smile*," and he brought the quartet back out and they did it. I am glad he didn't know me then; he might have turned J.D. loose on me!

My lifelong hobby and love has been The Blackwood Brothers Quartet and its spinoffs. My vocabulary is simply too limited to express properly the effect that they, and especially Mr. Blackwood, have had on my life. I am honored that he counts me as a friend.

Paul Heil

Paul Heil has the top syndicated gospel music radio show in America, called *The Gospel Greats*. Headquartered in Lancaster, Pennsylvania, Paul has long been a forceful advocate for Southern gospel music, and has used his radio program to promote gospel music and gospel singers for many years. Many singers and songwriters owe great debts to Paul for his efforts on behalf of the gospel music industry.

Aside from our common love of Southern Gospel music, James Blackwood and I share a love for radio. That, after all, has been my background for well over three decades.

Radio was also instrumental in making The Blackwood Brothers a household name during their earlier days. Indeed, radio played a big role in the early growth of Southern Gospel music. Here's how James recalled the early days of live radio programming during an interview for my syndicated radio program "The Gospel Greats":

"I enjoyed singing Gospel music on the radio much more than I ever have on television. There's something about radio. There's the mystique of it that really captures people's imaginations."

"For years, when we were on radio in Shenandoah, Iowa, during the winter months, we got mail regularly from 27 states and three Canadian provinces from our broadcast. The advertising people at the station estimated from the amount of mail we got—once we offered our photo to anyone who wrote in and we got ten thousand cards and letters in two weeks—that we probably had a million people listening to us every day."

Paul Heil

"When we went before that microphone and they gave us the 'on' signal, we knew that there were a million people out there listening to us. That did something to me and to us that neither television nor anything else has ever done."

James had another example of the power of radio in those days. He recalls the time when the Stamps-Baxter Music Company advertised songbook subscriptions in XERA, a 500,000-watt radio station just over the border in Mexico that broadcast directionally throughout the United States.

"I was in [Mr. Stamps'] office one morning when they brought the mail and the book orders in by trucks. That morning he had orders from 37 states and all the Canadian provinces, and even out into the ocean and the islands. So that was really putting Southern Gospel music on the map."

When asked about his favorite recollection, James will usually pass over the 1951 recording contract with RCA that made The Blackwood Brothers a nationally-known name. He will also usually not mention the 1954 appearance of The Blackwood Brothers on the Arthur Godfrey Talent Scouts show that gave the group additional recognition.

Instead, he admits people are usually surprised when he recalls something that happened in Veterans Memorial Auditorium in Greenville, South Carolina, at a concert which had drawn some 7,000 people.

As he tells it, "I was singing *I'll Meet You in the Morning*, and then, as I often do, I went off the stage down into the audience shaking hands with people along the front row. I went down an aisle as far as my microphone cord would let me, and people began coming down the aisle to shake hands. Suddenly I saw a little grey-haired lady coming down that aisle on crutches."

"She came to me with tears streaming down her face, put her arms around me and said, 'James, that's my promise to you. I'll meet you in the morning'."

"You know, that stays in my mind. And if I had to pick one thing that seems to have affected me more than any other—because she looked just like my little mother—that has to be number one in my life."

And that, I think, speaks volumes about James Blackwood.

Jake Hess

If James Blackwood has any equal as a lead singer, that man is Jake Hess. A member of the fabulous Statesmen Quartet for many years, Jake also formed The Imperials in the late 1960s and sang in the 1980s with The Masters V. A perennial star of the Gaither videos, Jake tours regularly in the Gaither concerts. His performances of songs such as *Then I Met the Master* and *Death Ain't No Big Deal* are among the many memorable moments his fans cherish. Few, if any, have ever equaled the showmanship and style of Jake Hess. He is a member of the Gospel Music Hall of Fame.

I could not possibly ever think of enough good things to say about James Blackwood. He has been my friend for more than forty-five years as we have shared stages from coast to coast. For many years, The Blackwood Brothers and The Statesmen were booked together in joint concert appearances, and neither of us could ever count the number of miles we have traveled together singing gospel music.

Later, in the 1980s, I sang with James as part of The Masters V, and my respect for him and my admiration for his character and accomplishments continued to grow. We have shared so many good times and sad times together that it is difficult to single out one or two incidents.

But I suppose that I will never forget that sad evening outside Clanton, Alabama, on June 30, 1954, when the plane crash occurred that took the lives of James' beloved nephew R.W. and Bill Lyles, one of the smoothest bass voices ever to grace the gospel music stage. As the plane burst into flames, many of us raced toward it to see if there was anything we could do. I recall realizing the hopelessness of the situation just about the time James rushed past me toward the wreckage.

Jake Hess

Almost without thinking, I grabbed James in full stride and picked him up as his feet were still flailing the air in his vain attempt to rescue R.W. and Bill. While I held him, he continued to kick as if he were still running. My shins were bruised for weeks afterward!

A little later, as the reality of the tragedy was fully realized, James asked me to call his brother Doyle and his pastor, the Reverend Jim Hamill, back in Memphis so that they might know what had happened before the news media picked up the story. James also wanted Reverend Hamill to begin to minister as quickly as possible to the families of R.W. and Bill.

That night, we (The Statesmen) put James in our car to drive him back to Memphis. It was the longest and saddest drive of my life. Many times during that trip, James said "I'll never sing again." Each time he said that, Hovie or I or someone else would say "Yes, you will, James. You must." But James was adamant that his career was over.

As we were getting close to Memphis, we kept urging James that he absolutely had to continue the ministry of The Blackwood Brothers. Finally, James blurted out, "Well, who would I get to sing bass?" I said "You'll get J.D. Sumner." For the first time since we left Clanton, James gave a little smile and a slight chuckle.

I guess I didn't know at the time what a prophet I would be. Within six weeks, James had reconstituted The Blackwood Brothers Quartet. Bill Shaw continued as tenor, while Cecil Blackwood, R.W.'s younger brother, became baritone, and James did indeed hire J.D. Sumner as the group's bass singer. The unmistakable sound of The Blackwood Brothers survived despite this horrible tragedy, and continued to thrive and prosper as other personnel changes occurred, as they do in all gospel groups.

I think I would not be exaggerating if I said that James Blackwood and I had the privilege to sing lead for the two most famous gospel quartets of all time. Although The Blackwoods and The Statesmen always tried to outsing and outdo each other on the stage, I can honestly say that there has never been one moment when James and I have felt anything toward each other except deep friendship and abiding respect. He is my friend, and I love him. I still cherish each time that we have been able to sing together, and I hope that we will have many more opportunities to do so in the future.

Jim Hill

Jim Hill was singing with The Golden Keys, a quartet based in Portsmouth, Ohio, when he first met James. Later, after The Blackwood Brothers bought the Stamps Quartet Music Company and reorganized The Stamps Quartet, Jim Hill sang tenor with The Stamps. Jim is a gifted songwriter, whose most famous hymn is probably *What A Day That Will Be*. Jim later sang with The Statesmen after his tour with The Stamps, and is a Minister of Music in Ohio.

Just mention the name of James Blackwood, and one immediately thinks of gospel music, because he IS Mr. Gospel Music. From small churches on the back roads near Shenandoah, Iowa, to the nation's largest coliseums, James and The Blackwood Brothers blessed the hearts of millions through their message in song.

I have been associated with James for more than 40 years, and have always found him to be compassionate and sincere. He has always been ready to go on stage, regardless of what personal pain or sorrow he may be experiencing. With his head back and flashing that winning smile, he stood tall. After his performances (and usually before), he always took time to talk to the fans and to listen sincerely to them.

All of us who have made a living in gospel music should understand that the true dedication and perseverance of James Blackwood in pioneering gospel music have made our careers possible. We should never forget that.

My life has been blessed for having known the greatest tenor in any field of music, sacred or secular. There will never be another James Blackwood. If there is, I hope he's my grandson.

Rex Humbard

Rev. Rex Humbard is one of the nation's best known evangelists, and has been for more than fifty years. He had one of the first (if not the first) regularly syndicated evangelistic television programs, called *The Cathedral of Tomorrow*. He and James are almost exactly the same age, with James celebrating his sixty-third year in gospel music and Rev. Humbard celebrating his sixty-third year as a minister of the gospel.

I met James Blackwood for the first time fifty-seven years ago. I had just come from Arkansas to work with Albert Ott at Bethel Temple and also with V.O. Stamps and his quartet. James and I attended a singing school at Oak Cliff together, and I'll never forget meeting him.

I was immediately impressed by his dignity and his talent in presenting the gospel of Jesus Christ through music and song. Down through all of these years since, I have admired James for all that he stands for, and for his attitude toward honesty and decency. He has been a real inspiration to me and a true friend.

James and I are not as young as we used to be, but that doesn't keep us from delivering the message that God has laid upon our hearts. This year, I am completing sixty-three years in the ministry since I did my first radio program as a thirteen-year-old boy in Hot Springs, Arkansas.

James' life has been almost the same as mine, for he is in his sixty-third year in full-time gospel music. All his life, he has told people about our Lord and Savior Jesus Christ. As we come to this time in our lives when we are nearing the end of our journey, I know that his desire along with mine is that we can hear "Well done, thou good and faithful servant."

On a lighter note, I wonder if James remembers those Shaw Sisters when we attended the singing school years ago. They created a real sensation at that time. I think we both took a good look at them, then a second look and a third look! But it was during that time some fifty-seven years ago that I met my wife, Maude Aimee, and we have now been married fifty-three years.

So James and I have a lot of memories, and we can both be grateful that the Lord has been our greatest friend. I know that James will continue to tell people about Jesus and will sing his praises all the days of his life. Thank you, James, for being my friend.

Rev. Humbard and his wife Maude Aimee with James at a National Religious Broadcasters convention in Washington, late 1970s.

Jerry Kirksey

Jerry Kirksey is Editor-in-Chief and Associate Publisher of *The Singing News*, the leading magazine of Southern gospel music. For more than thirty-five years, Jerry has been an active promoter and staunch advocate of quality gospel music. Through the pages of *The Singing News*, Jerry has drawn national attention to gospel music, and has played a major role in helping to advance the careers of many gospel singers. He is one of the most knowledgeable authorities on the history of Southern gospel music.

Even though I was new at working in Southern gospel music, I was a lifetime fan. I had heard of James Blackwood all of my life. When the time came for me to actually meet the man, my breath got short, my legs trembled, and I was overwhelmed. Then it happened. This legendary man stuck out his hand, a smile covered his face from ear to ear, his handshake was strong and his voice sincere: "Welcome to the National Quartet Convention, Jerry, and welcome to our business. I hear you really know radio. We need people like you. Come out and visit us at the record shop."

I could not believe my ears or my eyes. A man like James Blackwood saying to me "We need you," and "Come visit me." Needless to say, I was now an even bigger fan than before.

Over the past 36 years, James and I have become best friends. I am still in awe of this man. I still feel the same in his presence as I did that first time. James Blackwood has never in these 36 years ever done or said one thing that would make me bring him down from the pedestal I put him on in the beginning. To me, he is still Mr. Class. The epitome of taste and perfection, he can sit with kings and presidents and hold his own. Yet, he can minister to the lowliest of men with true compassion and understanding. James Blackwood is a majestic man driven by a servant's heart.

I am not sure which virtue James will be most remembered for: his awesome talent as a singer, or his unique ability to always be on stage, microphone in hand, and at the same time be a down-to-earth Christian man and a true friend—you know, kind of like your hero and your buddy all at the same time.

Jerry Kirksey

Hovie Lister

An ordained Baptist minister, Hovie Lister formed the famous Statesmen Quartet in 1948, which most scholars of Southern gospel music would consider The Blackwood Brothers' only peer. In 1952, The Blackwood Brothers and The Statesmen formed a quartet team which only added to the solo popularity which each group already enjoyed. In addition to being an outstanding singer and pianist, Hovie is considered one of the most astute businessmen in any field of music, and (with the possible exception of James) perhaps the finest quartet manager ever. He is a member of the Gospel Music Hall of Fame.

James Blackwood and I have been friends for more than forty years. I formed The Statesmen Quartet in 1948, and in the early 1950s, The Statesmen and The Blackwood Brothers formed a quartet team, which had never been done before in the history of gospel music. We played every date together, and we were the only two groups on the program as we filled buildings from coast to coast.

What a joy it was to work with James! He was the manager of The Blackwood Brothers, and people would call James to book The Blackwoods and he would also book The Statesmen. People would call me to book The Statesmen, and I would also book The Blackwoods. All we had to do was to pick up the telephone and call each other about the bookings.

One night we were booked in Alabama somewhere between Birmingham and Tuscaloosa, and I had failed to record that show in my date book. I was sitting at home in Georgia watching TV when James called. He said "Where are you?" I said "I'm home watching TV, where are you?" He said "We're over here in Alabama at our concert, and we're waiting for you." I said, "Well, I hope y'all enjoy it, 'cause we sure can't be there." In all the many years that James and I worked together, I think that was the only mixup we ever had about booking dates, so I guess that's pretty good.

One night we were singing in Dayton, Ohio, with the quartet team as usual. There was a gentleman named Walter who had booked us in that area who was a wonderful man, but had a habit of getting "into the spirit" if a quartet started singing a song that was very meaningful and spiritual. When this would happen, he would jump up and wave his hands at the audience and sit back down, and he usually sat on the front row. We had a bus driver named O'Neal Terry, who was really what I would call "goosey" or ticklish. You could just touch him or even just point at him and he would jump and jerk because he was so ticklish.

Well, late in the concert in Dayton, O'Neal came and sat beside Walter on the front row. We (The Statesmen) got into a song that was very fast and very inspirational, and Walter "got happy." He stood up and waved his arms at the crowd, sat back down, and grabbed O'Neal by the knee. This so startled and tickled O'Neal that he jumped up. Walter thought that O'Neal was in the Spirit too, grabbed him, and they both danced a jig together. We got so tickled onstage that we finally just couldn't finish the song and just quit even trying. I think it was the only time we ever just "quit."

I could tell many more funny stories that James and I have shared, but I want to be serious for a moment. All down through these years, James Blackwood has been a true friend. He has been faithful and loyal, a friend who calls to check on me, and encourages me when I've been down. I love him to death.

Hovie and James in the subway serving members of the U.S. Senate, Washington, D.C., mid-1960s.

But I'll never forget the sad, sad night when we were in Alabama when the plane crash occurred that took the lives of R.W. Blackwood and Bill Lyles. James rode back to Memphis that night with The Statesmen, and was so distraught and so sad, often saying "I'll never sing again." We all said "James, don't say that. That's Satan trying to discourage you. We're going to pray with you and for you and help you get through this." I have never seen such a distraught man as James was that horrible night.

But God has blessed him down through the years and has caused him to be a great, great blessing to hundreds of thousands of people, not just here in the United States, but all around the world. James has traveled this whole world, singing gospel music and proclaiming the name of Jesus Christ.

I love James Blackwood with all my heart.

Mosie Lister

When one thinks of the great gospel songwriters of the 20th century, names such as Albert E. Brumley, Bill Gaither, Stuart Hamblen, Ira Stanphill, and the incomparable Mosie Lister come immediately to mind. Songs such as *'Til the Storm Passes By, Where No One Stands Alone, His Hand In Mine,* and *How Long Has It Been?* have established Mosie in the forefront of songwriters. Mosie was a member of the original Statesmen Quartet when the group was formed by Hovie Lister in 1948. James describes Mosie as a "gentleman's gentleman."

James Blackwood has a great number of very fine qualities which I admire very much. He not only is an outstanding gospel singer and musician, but he is also devoted to his friends and to gospel music. My wife and I have known James since the early 1950s, and over the years that friendship has grown and deepened. We share ideas and hopes frequently.

James not only loves gospel music, but he wants it to be presented at its very best and has worked hard to do that and to present his music in a way which truly communicates with the listener. As a songwriter, I deeply appreciate the way he interprets songs, for he has presented a number of mine in an excellent fashion. He not only helped to make those songs known to the general public, but he sang them in such a way as to capture the attention of many younger singers who were just beginning their careers.

Two groups come to mind immediately which have been tremendously affected and influenced by James' approach to gospel music. Larry Gatlin and The Gatlin Brothers learned many of The Blackwood Brothers songs as very young boys in the 1950s, including songs of mine like *I'm*

Feelin' Fine and *His Hand In Mine.* They still sing many of them in their concerts, particularly *I'm Feelin' Fine.* The Statler Brothers were also heavily influenced by The Blackwood Brothers, and a few years ago made a new album of gospel songs in which they issued a new recording of *I'm Feelin' Fine.*

This is certainly testimony to the impact of James and The Blackwood Brothers that these two wonderful country groups still have such a deep love for gospel music and for its impact on their lives and careers.

I recall when The Blackwood Brothers went to New York in 1954 to sing on the Arthur Godfrey Talent Scouts program. I knew they were going, but I had no idea that they were going to sing two of my songs that week. But they did, and they were received very enthusiastically. Speaking strictly as a songwriter, I certainly appreciated that. It helped those songs become better known, and it was an honor to me that James and the quartet would select them.

James and the other members of the quartet would often come by our house when we lived in Atlanta. We would often spend some time around the piano singing, and I would try out some of my new songs on James. James always had an eye out for something new which would attract the attention of gospel music fans, and I treasure my memories of those occasions when we practiced new songs and arrangements.

The plane crash in 1954 which killed R.W. Blackwood and Bill Lyles might well have destroyed the quartet itself had it not been for James' determination that he still had a ministry to fulfill. He put the quartet back together, adding J.D. Sumner and Cecil Blackwood to the group. Even though these two new voices were very different than the ones they replaced, it is a testimony to James' professionalism and ability that he was able to maintain the sound and

Mosie Lister

style that The Blackwood Brothers had already established as the standard in the gospel music industry.

Perhaps James' main quality which I value and treasure so much is his constancy. Not only has the quality of his music been constant, but he has been consistent and constant with his friendship toward me and his attitude toward people in general. In all the years I have known him, I don't believe I have ever heard him say anything unkind or detrimental about anyone. He has always been interested in my songs and my songwriting career, and he has always been the same every time I have talked to him. Even as I write these lines, I am looking forward to seeing him again at the National Quartet Convention, where I hope we will be able to spend some "quality" time together talking about our old times in gospel music and the good future which the industry obviously has.

I truly appreciate all the things that James has done which have been a help to me over the years. He presented my songs to the public and certainly helped my career. He always made me feel as though in some way I was a part of what he did, and generously attributed at least some of his success to my songs.

If I could sum up James' qualities, I would simply say this: He is a constant and wonderful friend; he constantly strives for the best quality in what he does, always attempting to take a middle-of-the-road approach to gospel music which attracts fans from every spectrum; and he insists on "quality," not only in performing, but also in the way he lives his life. This characteristic has always had a significant impact on anyone who has ever come in contact with him. Many are the individuals and groups who have looked to James Blackwood as both a professional *and* a personal role model, and I certainly count myself among those. Having James for a friend is one of the greatest privileges my wife and I have ever had.

John McDuff

John McDuff sings lead with The McDuff Brothers, a noted gospel trio which also includes his brothers Coleman and Roger. He is an Assembly of God minister in Houston, Texas. James has great confidence in John McDuff and says that if he really needed someone to pray for him, John McDuff would be one of the first he would call.

I will never forget the first time I had the experience of seeing James Blackwood and The Blackwood Brothers Quartet perform in person. The announcer said "Ladies and gentlemen, I present to you James Blackwood and The Blackwood Brothers Quartet." Out on the stage walked a man, yet a living legend. There he was, no taller than I am, but he appeared to be ten feet tall. He was a regal image, doing what God called him to do.

How did it all begin for James and The Blackwood Brothers? From the deep South and from a family without many of the comforts of life came these anointed singers. I can identify with that, because it reminds me of our own humble beginnings (Coleman, Roger, and me).

We McDuff Brothers were reared by a grandfather who was a gambler and a drunkard. But we had a grandmother who knew how to pray. She prayed us all in, and we three little rascals became preachers and gospel singers. Our first experience as a singing trio came when we were kids. We had misbehaved, and Mama sent us to the bathroom to take a bath—all three of us in the tub at the same time. She stepped into the room with a switch and said "Boys, I want you to sing!" Sing we did, at the top of our lungs!

James and The Blackwoods were born to sing. God took James and his family and used them to make an impact

John McDuff

upon the gospel music industry that has never been rivaled. Only in eternity will we fully realize the fullness of that impact. Someone in that family knew how to pray!

Many will remember being touched when they saw the love that James and his family demonstrated toward James' parents. James and his brothers would lovingly bring their parents into the concert hall and place them in the most desired area so that they could hear and see their children sing. Surely in heaven the Lord has given them a special place so that they can still hear James and his current quartet continue to sing to the glory of God.

One particular scene will always stick in my mind, and it occurred at the National Quartet Convention some years ago in Memphis. The Blackwood Brothers and James were on stage singing *I'll Meet You In the Morning*, and it was powerful! The convention hall was absolutely full of people shouting and praising God. James moved down to the floor, stood on a chair, and continued to sing as only he can.

One of his sons turned to me and remarked, "I believe that's the way Daddy would like to go home to be with Jesus—surrounded by people who love him, standing on a chair, and singing *I'll Meet You In the Morning*." What a moving moment! It will remain in my memory forever.

I am so grateful to God for allowing James Blackwood to be my friend. Although I sometimes feel unworthy, to be loved and respected by James and to be called his friend is one of my life's greatest treasures.

Gary McSpadden

Gary McSpadden has had a long and varied career in gospel music. At an early age, he sang with The Statesmen, and later with The Oak Ridge Boys. He also was a member of The Bill Gaither Trio and The Gaither Vocal Band, and was an original member of The Imperials. With one of the more versatile voices in gospel music, Gary is equally at home singing lead or baritone. Headquartered in Nashville, Gary is a leading gospel music television producer, publisher, and executive.

I remember the first time I ever saw James Blackwood. It was at an old airplane hangar that had been converted into a makeshift auditorium at the Lubbock, Texas, airport. I was a nine-year-old kid who had no idea about some of the things that were going to change my life.

That night, The Blackwood Brothers, The Statesmen Quartet, and The Golden Gate Quartet sang their music and I was absolutely mesmerized. I had never seen that mixture of gospel music and entertainment before. To sing the music that James and R.W. Blackwood and Jake Hess sang became a dream for me. For at that moment—in that unlikely place—my dream was born.

Some time later, I remember my mother asking me what I wanted to be when I grew up, and that I said "a gospel singer." This was not particularly what she wanted to hear. She replied, "No, you know what I mean, I want to know what you want to do to make a living?" Whenever that question was asked, my answer was the same over and over again. It was because of what I saw on that stage at my first gospel concert where James, The Blackwood Brothers, and those other great gospel singers helped me decide what I wanted to do with my life.

I have been privileged to share the stage with James Blackwood on many occasions through the years. My entrance as a professional gospel singer was as a temporary replacement with The Statesmen Quartet while Jake Hess was in the hospital recuperating from a serious illness. I remember the first night when, as a nineteen-year-old, I stood between Rosie Rozell and Doy Ott and tried to sing Jake's part. Scared but trying, I think my knees were knocking together louder than I was singing. I remember James

Gary McSpadden

coming to me after the performance with kind words, telling me what a good job I had done. During those months, many people encouraged this "wet behind the ears" Texas teenager. These people have become my lifelong friends, especially Jake Hess and James Blackwood.

When Jake returned to sing with The Statesmen, I became part of The Oak Ridge Boys. During my years with "The Oaks," I got married to a beautiful girl named Carol. We were wed at the National Quartet Convention, and we asked James to stand in for Carol's father. I will be forever grateful to my dear friend James Blackwood for walking down the aisle and giving away (to me) my wonderful wife on that beautiful October Sunday afternoon.

James has always been and continues to be such a blessing to us. I am so thankful that he is my friend.

Buck Morton

Currently a pastor in Paris, Tennessee, Dr. Buck Morton has served for many years as the inimitable Master of Ceremonies at the National Quartet Convention now headquartered in Louisville, Kentucky. He has also been a minister for Baptist churches in Memphis and in Missouri.

Several anecdotes come to mind regarding my lifelong friend, Dr. James Blackwood. Frankly, I enjoy savoring each one. I recall the time at the National Quartet Convention (when it was still headquartered in Nashville) when James was the subject of a "roast" at the Holiday Inn Crown Plaza. Along with me at the head table were fellow-roasters such as Mosie Lister, J.D. Sumner, Bill Gaither, Hovie Lister, Bill Traylor, and Jake Hess. A favorite story I shared with the group occurred when James was about 19 or 20 working the quartet circuit in his native state of Mississippi. By this time, James was deeply in love with a beautiful young lady from Weathersby, Mississippi, named Miriam (Mim) Grantham. In those lean times for the quartet, James admitted that he was not only in love, but usually hungry all the time! Fortunately, Miriam's mother was a great cook, and when the quartet's only vehicle was available to James, he was usually off to Weathersby to visit Mim.

On one occasion when James was to visit Mim, the Blackwoods' car was not available, so James spent nearly all his money on a bus ticket from Jackson to Weathersby. He arrived at Mim's home happy to see her, but hungry as usual. Soon, however, he learned that Mrs. Grantham was not feeling well and that she had not prepared supper. But she had given permission for Mim and James to go out to eat.

Buck Morton and James.

"I was stunned," James confessed later. "The bus fare had pretty well cleaned me out, and I had less than twenty cents in my pocket. Mim ordered a sandwich and a soft drink in a small restaurant downtown. I told the waitress to go ahead and bring her order, but that I wasn't hungry. I reassured Mim that I was feeling fine except for a temporary loss of appetite. While she ate the sandwich, I was furiously trying to figure a graceful way out of this dilemma. Knowing that the moment of disgrace was close at hand, I closed my eyes as Mim motioned to the waitress to bring the check. I began to say 'Mim, I'm sorry, but . . . .' Then I opened my eyes to see Mim handing the waitress a dollar bill. At the same time, she said 'Mother was so sorry that she wasn't feeling well today and could not fix dinner for us. She gave me money to treat you, instead. I do hope you'll feel more like eating next time'."

Or there was the Saturday many years later when Dr. and Mrs. Blackwood visited our studios at WWGM (Wonderful World of Gospel Music) at Casey Jones Village in Jackson, Tennessee. As they parked in front of our studios and proceeded to walk in, the electronic alarm system in their new car went off, much to the embarrassment of both of them!

In October of 1989, I experienced an occlusion of the main artery in my heart and had to undergo cardiac catheterization and an angioplasty. One of the first to visit me in the intensive care unit of Baptist East Hospital in Memphis was my friend James Blackwood. In my more than 40 years as a minister, I have made hundreds of hospital visits, ministering to the needs of others. This time, it was my turn to be ministered unto.

My lovely wife Annette was with me when Steve Bradford and Dr. James Blackwood entered my room. Steve and Annette sat down on one side of my bed and James sat on the other. After a short conversation, I said to James, "I know you know how to get in touch with the Lord. Will you please pray for me, for my family, my church, and my ministry?" His response was "Yes," and indeed he did. This man of God reached heaven for me, and the Father heard and granted his petition on my behalf. I am healed, thanks to Prayer Warriors such as James Blackwood who interceded for me.

Only Eternity will reveal how much this godly man and his lovely companion have meant to multitudes, including my family. I am deeply honored and humbly grateful to be numbered among his many friends.

Rex Nelon

An outstanding and smooth bass singer, Rex Nelon sings with his family-based group, The Nelons. A native of North Carolina, Rex also sang with The Homeland Harmony Quartet and was a member of The LeFevres for many years. When Eva Mae LeFevre decided to quit touring, the group became known as The Nelons. James says that Rex Nelon "doesn't have an enemy in the world. Everybody likes Rex."

I have been traveling full-time in gospel music for 41 years, but that's not a drop in the bucket compared to James Blackwood's 63 years in the industry.

Rex Nelon

James is and has always been a true example of what a gospel singer should be, not only in the way he lives his life, but also in the way he promotes gospel music. No one in the industry works any harder than James does.

James has been blessed with one of the greatest voices in the history of gospel music, and as I have grown to know him better, I realize more and more what a great man he truly is. He would be the perfect example for any young gospel singer (or any young person) to pattern a life after.

One of the greatest honors of my life is to be able to say that James Blackwood is my friend. He is what gospel music is all about, and I love him like a brother.

Duane Nicholson

Duane Nicholson sings first tenor with The Couriers, one of the finest male trios in Southern gospel music. While attending Bible college in Springfield, Missouri, he often heard The Blackwood Brothers sing at the Shrine Mosque, which was a regular stop on the quartet's tour. He appears regularly on the Gaither videos, and is considered one of gospel music's true gentlemen.

The Blackwood Brothers were the first gospel group I ever heard. My father was pastor of a church in Woodbine, Iowa, when I was a teenager. The Blackwoods lived in Shenandoah, and they would come to Woodbine or the surrounding area a few times each year. Little did I know at that time that later on in life I would have the privilege of singing on the same stage with James Blackwood and The Blackwood Brothers, and that I would promote them many times in Harrisburg, Pennsylvania. I still consider James Blackwood one of the finest gentlemen I have ever known, even though he contributed to one of the most embarrass-

Duane Nicholson

ing moments in the history of gospel music. I know, because I was the victim!

James, along with Doug Oldham, Don Butler, Don Storms, Brock Speer, and others were guests on the PTL Club television program hosted by Jim Bakker and Henry Harrison. On this particular day, each of the guests was asked to tell about his most embarrassing moment on stage, or an embarrassing moment he had witnessed on stage. I was at home in Pennsylvania watching this live broadcast from Charlotte, North Carolina. I laughed along with everyone else as one by one the guests told their stories. As I watched and laughed, I was thinking "But none of these is as funny or as embarrassing as what happened to me."

Just as I was saying this to myself, Jim Bakker said "Well, these are all funny stories, but we haven't told the funniest one I have ever heard." He proceeded to tell the story about "one of The Couriers" going on stage with toilet paper stuck to the back of his pants trailing all the way down to his knees while he was trying to sing gospel music to 400 stunned people. Someone threw a roll of toilet paper onto the set at the PTL show, and someone else said "Maybe it's time we sang 'When the ROLL is Called Up Yonder'." Everyone was laughing, and Henry Harrison laughed so hard that he leaned back in his chair and fell over backwards right there on national television.

The capstone of the story came when someone asked which one of The Couriers was the victim of this incident, and Jim Bakker replied that he didn't know. I thought my identity and my pride were secure until James spoke up very loudly and said for millions to hear "Oh, I know which one it was. It was Duane Nicholson." Since that time, I have been asked about this event almost everywhere we have sung, and I have to recount the whole story detail by detail.

Thanks a million, James.

Squire Parsons

James says that Squire Parsons is respected as "a singer, a songwriter, and a gentleman." Before his current successful solo career, Squire sang lead with The Kingsmen. One of the most noted of contemporary gospel songwriters, his most famous song is probably the classic *Beulah Land*, which he mentions below. Like many others who emulate James, Squire is one of the best at the "stand-up-and-sing-flat-footed" style which James and The Blackwood Brothers made famous.

The longer I know James Blackwood, the more I'm impressed with his gift, his talent, and his integrity as a Christian. I had idolized him as a youth, but I never got to meet him personally until I joined The Kingsmen Quartet in 1975. During the four years I was with The Kingsmen, we sang with The Blackwood Brothers quite a few times. At one of those concerts (Chicago, I believe), a very humorous incident took place which I think of often.

Let me set up the story this way. In the 1970s, The Blackwoods and The Kingsmen were very much "performance oriented." By that I mean that both groups wanted to be a blessing in a spiritual sense, but there was also an air of competitiveness between the two groups for crowd response. Jim Hamill of The Kingsmen and Cecil Blackwood had been together in their youth and actually attended Bible college together, as I recall. They also sang some together and through the years had maintained a great friendship, tempered with a gracious competitiveness.

But on to my story. The Blackwoods were singing before The Kingsmen that night and *were* they ever singing! The group at that time consisted of the great Pat Hoffmaster, tenor; Jimmy Blackwood, lead; Cecil Blackwood, baritone; Ken Turner, bass; and Tommy Fairchild at the piano. James, however, did not sing during the opening part of the program. He came out about halfway through their stand.

Well, The Blackwoods were at their best and looked their best, dressed in their elegant black suits. I was standing backstage with the great emcee, stage manager, and lead singer of The Kingsmen Quartet, Jim Hamill. We were listening and observing their great performance. People were cheering, applauding, and whistling after every song. Then, all of a sudden, a deafening applause came from the audience as James Blackwood skipped across the stage in a beautiful white suit singing *I'll Meet You In the Morning*. Hamill looked at me and pulled the stage curtain back to see hundreds of people standing and cheering as James, with his white suit and angelic voice, continued singing as only he can.

After a few moments of watching, Hamill turned to me and said, "I believe these people have him (James) and God mixed up." I don't know when I have ever laughed so much and Hamill joined me in the laughter. We both watched in awe as the living legend James Blackwood continued to share his music and message that night. Hamill said, "He gave us all a singin' lesson tonight."

Another incident that I remember was a big encouragement for me. It was some years later when Hovie Lister and James were singing with The Masters V. I had started my own ministry and had joined them at a meeting somewhere. Hovie told me, "Squire, we want to do a song for you." I don't know that I have ever been more overwhelmed than I was when I heard James Blackwood begin to sing my song *Beulah Land*.

It was another—and for me very moving—"singing lesson."

Roy Pauley

Roy Pauley writes a regular column for *The Singing News*, and is an ardent and sometimes controversial advocate for quality in Southern gospel music. He believes that The Blackwood Brothers and The Statesmen set the standard for gospel quartets, and has little use for trendy experimentation with a proven medium. Roy has sung bass with The Weatherford Quartet and a number of other groups, and has an extensive ministry in the Seventh-Day Adventist Church.

It's funny how little insignificant happenings stick with us. At the 1991 "Grand Ole Gospel Reunion" in Greenville, South Carolina, James Blackwood and I ran into each other in the hallway just left of the stage. There were a lot of important people wandering around in the area. As James and I approached each other, I thought to myself "Here's my chance to be seen by all these folks chatting with THE James Blackwood." But after two or three seconds, James asked me where my wife Amy was. I told him she was sitting just around the corner against the wall just offstage. So he immediately turned on his heel to say hello to her, and I was left wondering what in the world happened to my chance to be seen casually chatting with a legend. I asked Amy later if James found her. She replied that he had, and that they had chatted for quite a while. I was jealous! But I must admit that I was indeed proud that James thought Amy was important enough to search her out that night in Greenville.

But I do find a bit of comfort and self-importance when I recall a Blackwood Brothers concert Amy and I attended a couple of years earlier in Bowling Green, Florida. James called me out of the audience to take his place on the great classic *How Great Thou Art.* To think that this man would sacrifice what was sure to be a huge response to this powerful song in order that I could sing it was an unbelievably kind and unselfish gesture. And by the way, it's something he's never asked Amy to do!

I saw James Blackwood for the first time about 1955 in my home town of Charleston, West Virginia, at a church called the Union Mission. James hit the stage singing *Heavenly Love,* and I'll never forget it. Since then, I suppose I've seen him in concert at least seventy-five times. As a child of six or seven, I sensed that James Blackwood was something extraordinary. I've always marveled at his voice and the things he could do with it. As a singer, James could do more with his voice than probably any other singer who

Roy Pauley

ever lived. He could always give the big, robust sound, of course, but he could also give the sweet, soft touch as well. Raring back and letting those big tones flow is what he's best known for, but that's not all there is to James Blackwood's singing. He has taught us that true singing is an art form—a thing of beauty.

I've watched him carefully through the years and I've observed his constant professionalism. I've always been impressed with his willingness to mix with his admirers. When The Masters V was formed in the early 1980s (with James, Hovie, Jake, J.D., and Rosie), someone supposedly came up with the idea that the group should stay out of sight of the audience until the very moment they walked onstage. I've heard that James spoke up and told the others in the group that they could stay hidden from the crowds if they wanted to, but that he was going to make himself available to the people. Now I'm unable to verify this conversation, but it does sound like something James would say. As anyone who has attended one of James' concerts can attest, James can always be found mixing with the people beforehand, willing and anxious to meet with his fans.

James Blackwood is a legend among legends. He and the fabulous Blackwood Brothers truly helped revolutionize Southern gospel music in every imaginable facet. Their recordings from the 1940s through the 1960s will go down in history as true classics, and should serve as textbooks for those who would seek to know what true quartet singing should sound like.

. Thank you, James, for more than sixty-three years of skillful singing, and for teaching us what professionalism, durability, and commitment really are. But more than that, thank you for treating each of your fans with kindness and respect. As long as time lasts, these contributions will be your legacy.

Glen Payne

Glen Payne has sung lead for The Cathedral Quartet for more than thirty years, and he has been singing gospel music professionally for more than forty years. Like George Younce, The Cathedrals' bass singer, Glen also sang with The Weatherford Quartet early in his career. Most fans and observers of Southern gospel music would rank Glen as the most outstanding quartet lead singer active today. Although The Cathedrals have had several tenors and baritones through the years, Glen's distinctive lead voice and George's bass singing have combined to give The Cathedrals a remarkably consistent sound. A fan favorite, The Cathedrals are equally at home with convention-type songs and those with more contemporary melodies and messages.

James Blackwood has been my friend for more than forty years. I have always admired his singing and the integrity

Glen Payne and James.

he brings to our profession, as well as the remarkable lon-
gevity of his career.

More than that, James is truly a *good* man. He has
brought a lot of credit to the gospel music industry, and I
am certain that he always will. I am honored and happy to
have him as a friend.

Naomi Sego Reader

Naomi Sego Reader sang alto with one of the most famous mixed quartets of all time, The Sego Brothers and Naomi, which she describes below. Her group is today called The Segos, and she continues to tour regularly. Naomi is a regular on the Gaither videos, and James says that Naomi "is a sweet lady—everybody loves Naomi."

Just a short time after I married James Sego (a quartet man himself) on March 2, 1949, I became acquainted with most of the famous gospel quartets of that period, includ-

Naomi Sego Reader

ing the famous Blackwood Brothers. My husband's group, "The Harmony Kings," consisted of W.R. Sego, Charlie Norris, Lamar Sego, my husband James, Charlie Norris, Jr., with Lelia Norris (Charlie's mother) at the piano. They would help in the promotion of the all night "sings" sponsored by the Macon (GA) Fire Department and Chief Virgil King. The Harmony Kings would often open for The Blackwood Brothers, and I would be in the audience feeling very proud of my husband and his group.

Little did I realize at that time that I would become a part of the gospel music industry myself and have the honor of sharing the same stage with such great singers as James Blackwood. I appreciate the fact that James Blackwood has created history in the gospel music field, and I know that he will leave behind a legacy that will be admired and followed by others for generations to come.

I love James Blackwood and his wonderful singing and great testimony for the Lord. We've sung together many times down here, and I know we are going to sing forever up there.

Ray Shelton

Ray Shelton sang with The Senators Quartet for about fifteen years, and is to be thanked (along with Brad White) for convincing James to form a new quartet in 1990. Ray sings baritone with The James Blackwood Quartet, and is in the bus-leasing business in Memphis. Among his recordings is *Ray Shelton and the Legends*, which features Ray singing with J.D. Sumner, Jake Hess, and James.

In all my years of traveling in gospel music, James Blackwood is the easiest person to travel with I have ever encountered. When a problem arises, James is always very calm and is able to come up with a solution that satisfies everyone involved.

Ray Shelton

I have a lot of stories and anecdotes that I remember about James. I'll tell just three. Once, we had a bus driver who was only about 20 years old. When James was introducing all of us from the stage, he said that he had known our bus driver "all of *my* life."

On a recent tour to the west coast which lasted about three weeks, James lost his voice about midway through the tour. All he could do was whisper, so we decided to play tapes and lipsync the songs. After the concert, we had many people come up to our merchandise table to ask how in the world James could sing so well and not be able to talk.

Finally, I remember another night when an old gentleman who had to be at least ninety years old came up after one of our concerts and said to James, "Young fella, I've been listening to you sing all of my life."

Life is never dull on the road with The James Blackwood Quartet!

Marion Snider

Marion Snider is one of the most famous pianists in Southern gospel music. He was pianist for the original Stamps Quartet. He played piano for The Blackwood Brothers for several months in 1940, and later formed a quartet called The Imperials. When Jake Hess later formed a group with the same name years later, he called Marion to ask permission. Marion appeared on one of the most recent Gaither videos, and clearly has not lost a thing in sound or style.

Anytime anyone asks me to say anything about James Blackwood, that's just like saying "Sic 'em!" to Fido, because I've always liked to talk about James. I've met lots of people in gospel music, but my favorite has always been The Blackwood Brothers Quartet, except (of course) for the original Stamps Quartet, which was my beginning in gospel music.

James and I have had a lot of fun together, and in my opinion, we did a lot of good singing together. We made a lot of people happy with our music. I know that all the people who love gospel music have the name of James Blackwood stamped indelibly on their hearts.

James Blackwood is a dear friend of mine, and I love him as much as all his fans.

Brock Speer

Brock Speer sings bass with The Speers, organized as The Speer Family by Mom and Dad Speer in 1921. Brock first sang with the group when he was five years old in 1925, and is one of the truly beloved gentlemen in Southern gospel music. Without question, The Speers have been one of the finest and most famous mixed groups in gospel music's history. Many young singers, especially female singers, got some of their most important training as a member of The Speers. The Speers have always stood for maintaining the quality and tradition of Southern gospel quartet singing.

As he has done his entire life, James Blackwood continues to sing Southern gospel music at every opportunity. His career has steadily grown until he is the epitome of lead singers in his field of music.

James, Glen Payne, J.D. Sumner, Brock, and Les Beasley.

He is known world-wide through radio, records, and television. The happiness and joy he has created with his unique vocal sound will be remembered for years to come.

The world is a better place because of James Blackwood.

The Statler Brothers

The Statler Brothers (Harold Reid, Phil Balsley, Jimmy Fortune, and Don Reid) have been the nation's premier country music vocal group for more than thirty years, and have won more awards than any other act in the history of country music. Since 1991, they have had a weekly television show on The Nashville Network. Their seemingly endless list of hits includes *I'll Go to My Grave Loving You, Elizabeth, Do You Know You Are My Sunshine?, The Class of '57,* and *Flowers on the Wall.* Early in their career, they were a gospel group called The Kingsmen. They close each of their TV shows with a gospel song, and have recorded five all-gospel albums. They maintain a standard of decency, class, and quality in country music which is unmatched.

Our very earliest memory of Southern gospel music was of James Blackwood. Three of the four of us grew up Presbyterians, and you just don't get much foot-stompin' Southern gospel music in the Presbyterian Church. About as wild as we get is maybe *Onward Christian Soldiers* with a waltz beat on an electronic organ; not exactly an "all night sing" atmosphere.

But we had a radio and we picked up a lot of all-night stations and early morning programs that featured gospel quartets. We're talking the early '50s here, and by this time The Blackwood Brothers were synonymous with the words gospel quartet. Even though we were just kids, that June night in 1954 when we heard on the radio that there had been a plane crash and that R.W. and Bill Lyles had been killed is still a vivid memory, one that will stick with us forever. We were stunned and shocked even though they were just names and voices to us. We had never seen their faces, but they were still a part of our lives. We knew their songs

The Statler Brothers—Jimmy Fortune, Harold Reid, Don Reid, and Phil Balsley.

and their spirits and felt a loss that a bunch of kids couldn't quite explain or even understand.

The first time we had the opportunity to put faces with those famous voices was a couple of years later at a National Guard armory in a little town about 25 miles down the road from us. The Blackwood Brothers were coming!! And we were going. And that thrill of first seeing James Blackwood lead his quartet on that small square stage and take command of an audience that was sitting there just daring someone to entertain them was an unmatched emotion to this day. From that night on, we knew what we wanted to do. We wanted to sing; to have a quartet. Our destiny was planned, if not necessarily determined.

We clapped and whistled and yelled for more, and when they took a break we stood by the record stand and bought all the albums, singles, and pictures we could carry and more than we could afford. There was Cecil and Wally and Bill and J.D. and, of course, James singing to us and James talking to us between the songs in that hypnotic Mississippi clip that made every baby hush, every kid sit still, and every old man and old woman listen and lean forward for the next word that would rush from his mouth and tie one song to the next as only he can. He charmed us from the stage, was kind to us at the record table, and generous to us when we asked for all that merchandise to be signed. He was a gentleman and a hero, and we wanted to be just like him.

Years later, we wrote all of this down in a song called *The Blackwood Brothers by The Statler Brothers.*

Through the years, we have gotten to know James on a personal basis. We went to other Blackwood concerts. He came with The Masters V and guested on a TV special with us. He and The Masters V stopped by our offices one day in Staunton, Virginia, and spent the afternoon with us. And while they were there, on our request, they gathered around an old upright piano we have there in our music room and sang a song for us; James leading a quartet of our heroes right there in our office, and this time they really were singing just for us. And we never walk by that old piano whether in the light of a busy business day or in the quiet of night if we're in there working alone that we can't hear James and Hovie and Jake and J.D. if we just stop and listen real close.

But the ultimate thrill was a recent appearance on our TV show by James alone. We close every one of our TV shows with a hymn or an old gospel song. It's a spot we reserve strictly for ourselves and no one ever sings the final song with us; not until James came. We invited him and asked him to sing the closing gospel song with us, and he most graciously said "Yes." So that night, after all these years, those four little boys who sat on the front row of the National Guard Armory and clapped till their hands swelled and who spent allowances way into next month at the record table, stood there on stage on television and sang *I Want To Be More Like Jesus* with James Blackwood.

Now we're ready to die.

Gordon Stoker

Gordon Stoker has sung lead with The Jordanaires for more than forty-six years. A truly unique quartet, The Jordanaires are one of the few groups equally at home with gospel and country music. Too, the quartet is famous not only in its own right, but as a backup group for many famous solo artists. As is the case with most groups, personnel changes have occurred often through the years, but Gordon Stoker's classic lead style continues to knit together the group's distinctive sound.

James Blackwood and I began our careers in gospel music when we were both teenagers. He was singing with his brothers Roy and Doyle and his nephew R.W., while I was playing piano for the John Daniel Quartet. Our paths crossed many times in the 1940s at various singing conventions and concerts.

I joined The Jordanaires in 1950 at about the time The Blackwood Brothers were about to hit their peak as one of the nation's most famous gospel quartets. The Jordanaires and The Blackwood Brothers ran into each other many times on the road in the 1950s, 1960s, and 1970s, and James always met me with a smile whenever he saw me. He still does, and I must say that I have never met anyone who enjoyed his work more than James Blackwood enjoys singing gospel music and being around others who love it as much as he does.

James and I have shared many happy moments together, and I will always treasure these experiences and my friendship with him.

J. D. Sumner

If one looks up "bass singer" in the dictionary, J.D. Sumner's picture will be next to it. J.D. joined The Blackwood Brothers in August of 1954, and sang with the quartet until 1965. Since that time, he has been the keystone of The Stamps Quartet, and also sang with The Masters V during the 1980s. He and The Stamps backed Elvis Presley for many years. J.D. has been a pioneer in the creation of the Southern Gospel Music Hall of Fame, as well as other gospel music organizations. A member of the Gospel Music Hall of Fame, J.D.'s prowess as a bass singer is unmatched, and his low range is admired (probably even envied) by other bass singers. Harold Reid of The Statler Brothers, a great bass in his own right, once playfully declined to participate in a "bass-off" suggested by Ralph Emery, replying that "Up beside J.D., I'm a tenor!" James is fond of saying that "J.D. will never live to be as old as he looks now."

James Blackwood means so much to me that if I start saying anything really serious about him, I'll get to crying and sniffling, so I think I will just tell a funny story or two. But I will say this: I've got a brother, and he's not any closer to me than James Blackwood is.

When I was with The Blackwood Brothers, I was the one who was supposed to tell a joke on stage whenever James' singing wasn't quite up to par. One night in Little Rock I told about the time I got on an elevator at the fourteenth floor and told the girl who was operating the elevator than I wanted to go to the bottom floor. She put the elevator in high gear and we hit the bottom floor with a thud and I let out a groan. "Did I stop too quick for you?" she said. "No," I said, "I always wear my britches down around my ankles."

Well, this time I didn't get the story quite right. I said that when the elevator hit the bottom floor the *girl operator*

J. D. with Brenda Dennis (Allen's wife) after a concert in Oklahoma City in November, 1996.

let out a groan. Then I said to her, "Did it stop too quick for you?" She said, "No, I always wear my britches down around my ankles." The crowd started laughing and I turned to James and said "What's wrong?" James said, "You fool, you've got the girl with HER britches down around her ankles!"

One night in Houston there was another story I didn't get quite right. Bill Shaw had written a song called *I'm Thankful* that had a recitation in it. I always liked to try to do the recitations, and so I was doing this one. I was supposed to say that "Whenever I've needed anything from the Lord, I've always called on him and he's always supplied my every need." But this time I said "Whenever the Lord has ever needed anything, He's always called on me, and I've always supplied His every need." James jumped in and said, "Whoa, whoaa-aa-aa. J.D., you're not supplying the Lord's needs. You're supposed to say he's supplying YOUR needs." I never did that recitation again after that night.

There are a lot of people who say that James Blackwood

may be the greatest gospel singer of all time. I don't know about that, but I do know that he is the greatest merchandise seller of all time. When I was with The Blackwood Brothers, I used to say that we might could have sung better if James had rehearsed us singing more instead of rehearsing us in record selling.

Anyhow, the way I figure it is this: When James dies and people are walking by to view the body, his wife Mim will be at the foot of the coffin with a tape rack saying "Here's James' latest releases, $10 each or three for $25." Then, at the head of the coffin, Cecil will be standing with a family Bible, saying "If you want to go to where Uncle James is, this book will tell you how to get there. Just $5 down and $5 a month."

James put it in his will that way, I think.

Cecil Todd

Cecil Todd has a nationwide ministry called "Revival Fires," and is headquartered in West Branson, Missouri. Formerly, the ministry's headquarters were in Joplin, Missouri. He has been very influential in missionary work in Russia, and has traveled widely in that area. He is one of the nation's best-known missionaries, and perhaps no one else has done as much work in Russia as has Rev. Todd.

My story about James happened in 1963. I was the minister of a church in Clayton, Oklahoma, a small town of about 650 located in the heart of the Kiamichi Mountains of southeast Oklahoma. I located there after burning myself out doing ten years of extensive evangelistic traveling.

I had started the church as the result of a big tent crusade I had held there in 1960. The attendance at this revival averaged 850 per night with a high of 3500. Since I loved gospel music, I had invited The Statesmen, The Chuckwagon Gang, The Oak Ridge Boys, and The Prophets Quartet to join me as our special singing guests in many of our citywide crusades.

After settling my family in Clayton when I became pastor there, I organized my own quartet, which we called "The Singing Rangers." As a special treat to this new group, on one occasion I took them to a quartet convention at the old Ellis Auditorium in Memphis to hear the famous Blackwood Brothers quartet. It was a nine-hour trip from Clayton to Memphis, and six of us were stuffed into a 1962 Pontiac Bonneville! We arrived just in time for the concert, and didn't even take time to eat.

My quartet had listened to The Blackwood Brothers many times on record, and we often tried to imitate their platform style. The rest of the guys were just as excited as I was to hear and see them in person, and we were not disappointed. We were so enraptured by their singing; none of us had ever witnessed anything like it, for they were even better in person than on record.

We had to leave the Ellis Auditorium about midnight to return home. We drove hard all night to get back, for some of us had to go to work early the next morning - without sleep. Our group was never the same after that experience. Our singing style and platform presence were changed dramatically, and my admiration and appreciation for The Blackwood Brothers has never wavered.

I am proud to say that James Blackwood has been my close friend and point of inspiration for more than 30 years. Over the years, James has made numerous appearances in our Revival Fires crusades, at rallies, on TV specials, and in our conferences. In my opinion, he is one of the most respected and admired gospel singers of this century.

Alden Toney

Alden Toney, originally from West Virginia, first met James when the quartet was operating from Shenandoah, Iowa, and Alden was living in Detroit. He began singing in The Toney Brothers Quartet, and probably introduced James to *Lead Me to That Rock*. Alden joined The Blackwood Brothers Quartet as first tenor in 1949 and sang with them until 1951. He later served many different automobile dealerships as an accountant and a bookkeeper.

I first met and heard The Blackwood Brothers (James Blackwood, R.W. Blackwood, Bill Lyles, Cat Freeman, and Hilton Griswold) in June of 1949 when they came to Detroit for their first appearance ever in Michigan. Their quartet was superior to any I had ever heard.

I was singing in a local quartet in Detroit, and after the program The Blackwood Brothers came out to our home, where we sang together. We were blessed by the singing and the testimony of The Blackwood Brothers. The gospel music fans of the Detroit area commented for months afterward that The Blackwood Brothers quartet was the best quartet they had ever heard.

In August of 1949, about two months later, I received a letter from James Blackwood inviting me to join The Blackwood Brothers quartet as first tenor. Cat Freeman had decided to leave the group to go back to his home in South Carolina.

Needless to say, I was excited. Within about two weeks, I joined The Blackwood Brothers in Shenandoah, Iowa, where they were based at that time. In these intervening 47 years, James Blackwood has become like a brother to me.

Alden
Toney

My first performance with The Blackwood Brothers was at a concert in northern Missouri, and we came back to Shenandoah in the wee hours of the morning. James was driving and I was the only other person in the car who was awake. James drove to his house, left the car running, got out and went inside. I thought he would be back in a few minutes because he didn't say "good-night" or "see you in the morning at the radio station," or anything like that. After sitting there for about five minutes wondering what was going on, I awakened Bill Lyles. Bill simply got behind the wheel of the car, drove to his house, and did the same thing. Then I woke up Hilton Griswold and he drove to his house and got out. That left me and R.W. still in the car. I awakened R.W., and then *he* drove the car to my hotel and let me out. Then R.W. drove himself home.

It took me a while to figure out that this was the regular mode of operation for the quartet. Everyone knew what was going on, and they didn't think they had to explain it to me!

We did not have a radio announcer on our program in Shenandoah. An engineer simply put us on the air and James took it from there. I was always impressed when a news bulletin would come in to the station, and the engineer would hand it to James to read. James was a combination newsman, announcer, and lead singer!

I cherish the time I spent as a member of The Blackwood Brothers quartet. Some of the most enjoyable times of my life occurred during that time. James is not only a legend as a singer, but also a legend as a friend. He always has time for people, no matter what their station in life. I count him not only a friend but as close as a brother.

Jack Toney

Jack Toney is referred to by James as a "singer's singer." He has been a member of The Statesmen Quartet for many years, and has written a host of songs which have become major hits for various Southern gospel groups. A true song stylist in the tradition of classic gospel singers, Jack now lives in Boaz, Alabama.

As a young boy growing up in the rural area of Northeast Alabama called "Sand Mountain," I spent a great deal of time listening to gospel music in its heyday—the 1940s and 1950s. I was fortunate to grow up in a Christian home and to attend regularly the Baptist church in our little community. There, I sang the old hymns of the church. In addition, my "Uncle Jimmy" was a regular teacher in the old-time singing schools, and I attended many in those days. It was there in that little community that my career began as a member of the high school quartet.

I was a faithful listener to local radio, and although many of my contemporaries were caught up in the Grand Ole Opry, my pleasure came from the wonderful sounds of the great gospel quartets of the day. My favorites were the "sensational" Statesmen and their only parallel, The Blackwood Brothers.

Although as a young man I listened with wonder to The Statesmen, I paid close attention to The Blackwoods, and in particular to the wonderful voice of James Blackwood. As I remember those days, I am sure that I might have used a word the young people use today if I were to describe my feelings about James Blackwood: "Awesome!"

I truly enjoyed The Blackwood sound. I thought their

Jack Toney

song selections were top-notch, and they had wonderful arrangements. James Blackwood quickly became my idol. I so admired his singing ability—his range, his quality, and clarity—that I began to pattern my singing after his. I've never been sorry that I chose to do so.

Later, when I was fortunate enough to join Hovie Lister and The Statesmen, I came to know James Blackwood personally, because The Statesmen and The Blackwoods regularly made joint appearances. I found Mr. Blackwood to be truly worthy of the admiration I felt for him. James Blackwood was and is the real gentleman he appears to be. He and Mim are a wonderful couple, and two of the nicest people I've ever known in the music industry. During those bygone days of traveling together, James was always very kind to me. He was always my contemporary and never acted in a condescending manner toward me. He became my close friend and, I am happy to say, still is.

A few years ago at an outdoor singing near Birmingham, James and I stood together in mud up to our shoetops after a beautiful Sunday afternoon had yielded to a 30-minute downpour. A tent covered the stage and the concert seating, but our merchandise tables had been set up just outside the tent.

James and I, along with others, stood talking near the tables, waiting our turns to go onstage. Suddenly, a gust of wind caught the tent and it rippled, sending several gallons of cold water down on our heads and backs. The emcee then began his introduction of James Blackwood. James turned to take one look at the soaked merchandise tables, shook himself briskly to shed as much water as possible, and took the stage. I have never witnessed such professionalism and dedication.

As part of the festivities at the 1995 Grand Ole Gospel

Reunion in Greenville, South Carolina, James donned a dress, lipstick, and makeup as part of a "Let's Make a Deal" skit. An unsuspecting Hovie Lister was called in and was surprised to find James in this outrageous costume claiming to be one of Hovie's former girlfriends. I am certainly glad that Hovie was there that day, because James told me that if Hovie had not showed up, he was going to announce that he was one of *my* ex-sweethearts!

I do not remember the specific occasion nor the reason which prompted the statement, but something James once said to an audience has really stuck with me as a method of living and coping with whatever comes along in this life. He simply said, "I refuse to be offended." I often think of that, and when little things happen to me, I also try to refuse to be offended.

James Blackwood has been one of the people who has made a difference in my life, and I'll always love and respect him. It is truly an honor to call him my friend.

Ken Turner

A native of South Carolina, Ken sang bass with such quartets as The Palmetto State Quartet and The Dixie Echoes before joining The Blackwood Brothers in the early 1970s, where he remained until the late 1980s. When James organized The James Blackwood Quartet, Ken and James were once again reunited. In addition, Ken has his own solo ministry when he's not active with The James Blackwood Quartet. James says that there's "something wrong with anyone who can't get along with Ken Turner."

James Blackwood—this is the name that for seventy-seven years has meant "faithful friend" and "consummate performer." As the Scriptures say, "Greater love hath no man than this, that he would lay down his life for his friend," but that describes what James would do.

I have sung with James for twenty-five years, traveling all across the United States and Canada, and into forty-five other countries. Who would have thought that this skinny kid from South Carolina would be able to fulfil a dream of singing with James Blackwood? My dream began in 1954, after watching The Blackwood Brothers on the Arthur Godfrey Talent show. I had already been listening to them for several years on the radio, and was a devoted fan. After hearing them on television that night sing *Have You Talked to the Man Upstairs?*, I began praying that one day my dream would come true. In 1971, it did. James called me and offered me the job singing bass with The Blackwood Brothers. It was one of the greatest moments of my life.

It was early in my first year traveling with the quartet that I learned a great truth. Inside a fully-grown, well-respected man can hide an impish little boy. James is a practical joker like none other. In other words, never keep your back to James too long: it could be dangerous.

The practical jokes started simply enough. It all began with a request. I asked James to bring me my shaving kit because he was going out to our bus to get his shaving kit. A few minutes later, he returned, threw my shaving kit on the floor, and slid it across the room to me. I snatched it up off the floor, and stomped into the bathroom. I slammed the door, letting him know I was upset, for I thought that surely everything inside was broken.

Instead, it was full of rocks. I could hear James laughing through the bathroom door. He thought he was so clever, but never knew that a payback was being planned.

Now it was my turn. After the service that evening, I got to the bus before James. I carefully pulled back the covers on his bunk and poured a "shaving kit" full of rocks in the middle of his bed, carefully returning the sheets to their place. I jumped in my bunk, pretending to be asleep. That night, James climbed into bed, not pulling the sheets far enough down to reveal the rocks. A few seconds later, he jumped out of bed so fast that he slipped and fell flat on his rear end while our bus rang with laughter. As happy as I was with my "payback," I knew that it would soon be my turn again.

It wasn't long after the "rock & roll" incident that he started his tricks again. While having breakfast together, we usually shared a newspaper to keep up with the world as we were traveling. As I held the paper, my view of James was blocked: big mistake. With my next sip of coffee, I found that my cup was full of salt. The next morning, as James read the paper, his view of me was blocked. With his next sip of coffee, he found that his cup contained a plastic cream container floating around like a buoy. I thought it would all end there, but it didn't.

One day while I was using the telephone, I should have

kept my eyes on James. While I was preoccupied, he had untied my shoe and tied the shoelace to the table leg. When I stood up to leave, I fell flat on my face. James rolled with laughter; come to think of it, the whole room did.

But I got my revenge. As we've traveled together over the years, we usually get one hotel room in which we all take shifts getting ready. Of course, we basically lived on the bus, but it was more convenient to have one large hotel or motel room where we could get ready. James and I were the early risers and usually got to the room first. While he showered, I squirted shaving cream onto the telephone ear-piece. When James got out of the shower, Pat Hoffmaster, our tenor, sneaked down to the lobby and called our room. Needless to say, James got an "earful" that morning!

Another time, James set his briefcase down beside a tele-phone. I wrapped the telephone cord around the briefcase handle and waited quietly. James got up and walked away. After about ten steps, James kept going but the briefcase came back.

On long trips, men can get a little "stir-crazy" on the bus. To break up a long west coast trip, I had a little fun. I set my wristwatch alarm to go off at 3:00 a.m. and put the watch in James' shoe. It went off, and so did he. He shot straight up and began tearing his bunk apart trying to find the annoying sound. I laughed so hard that I nearly rolled out of my bed. Picture the dignified, debonair James Blackwood in his undershorts, throwing shoes, socks, and underwear all over the bus. Well, maybe not!

Twenty-five years of practical jokes, of laughter, of boy-ish fun . . . that is the side of James Blackwood that many people do not see. There's a twinkle in his eye when he is up to something - a part of him that is the boy who never grew up. It makes him a wonderful friend and a joy to be around. You can never guess what he'll be up to next.

When I examine his life, James stands above almost anyone else I know. There are so many who talk the talk in gospel music, but not so many who walk the walk. I've seen him so sick that he could hardly walk, yet as soon as he stepped on stage, a renewed strength would come upon him that could only be the anointing of the Lord. He will go into the crowd and shake the hand of every person there, letting them know that he was grateful that they came. In my forty years of singing gospel music, I've never seen anyone else do that. But that's James.

The Bible says "Bear ye one another's burdens, thus fulfilling the law of Christ," and also "By this shall all men know that you are my disciples, when you have love one for another." These words must be written on James Blackwood's heart. My wife Judy and I can testify to this truth. A few years ago, we faced a financial crisis in which we quite possibly could have lost our home. One day our phone rang and it was James. He said "I'm your friend, and I'm here to help you." He informed us that he was mailing us a check the next day and that we could pay him back when we were able. Many people can claim to be true friends, but few put those feelings into action. But James does.

James has sung for Presidents and met royalty. He's won countless awards. He's a friend of Billy Graham and Jimmy Carter, yet a little grandma in a country church is just as important to him. He is my best friend and my spiritual mentor. He gave a skinny kid from South Carolina his greatest dream.

There aren't many people who can boast of the number of friends that James can. Few have known his level of success and victory, as well as heartaches that have made him stronger and trials that have made him wiser. Not many people can smile in the face of the Enemy. But that's James.

Wally Varner

Probably no one in the history of Southern gospel music has been a better piano showman than Wally Varner, and his performances on some of the Gaither videos attest to that fact. Wally played piano for The Blackwood Brothers at the height of their popularity in the 1950s and 1960s, and later developed business interests in Kentucky Fried Chicken franchises. He lives now in Winter Haven, Florida, where he maintains a successful mail-order business in gospel recordings and videos. In regard to one of Wally's anecdotes below, Jake Hess says that "Wally will eat gravy on ice cream if he thinks he can get away with it."

I think my first story about James might be called "James' most embarrassing moment." We (the quartet and I) had looked forward for some time to dining in the governor's mansion with Governor Jimmie Davis in Baton Rouge. We all wanted to be at our best, and it was evident that Governor Davis wanted to be at *his* best. He had the table beautifully set, with elegant waiters and security people all around. Certainly we all felt as if we needed to be on our P's and Q's.

Anyway, when it came time for dinner, we were seated at a really long table that would probably hold twenty or so. Governor Davis was seated at the head of the table with James just to his left. J.D. was seated just to the right of Governor Davis, and I sat next to J.D. I think Bill Shaw sat on my right. Cecil sat next to James.

Well, most of us didn't know much about politics, but James did and we pretty much let him carry the conversation for the rest of us. James and Governor Davis were really having a deep conversation about politics. It was all pretty formal for us.

Wally Varner

We had a very distinguished looking waiter, dressed in white tie and tails, and he was serving our table so graciously and in such a dignified manner. All the guys in the quartet knew that I loved gravy on potatoes, meat, or practically anything. Gravy was always my weakness, and I always asked for more practically anywhere we were.

J.D. noticed that my gravy supply was running low, and in that voice that could rattle the whole dining room and almost knocked James out of his seat, he rumbled at the waiter: "Hey, bring this man some more gravy." The waiter brought the gravy, but I was so embarrassed that I wouldn't put any more gravy on my plate. I was beginning to worry that James might fire both of us.

When J.D. saw that I wasn't going to take any gravy, he

took it on himself to really cover my potatoes with gravy as he dipped ladle after ladle onto my plate. Finally, I took his arm and pushed it away. Then I took the ladle and started filling his plate up with gravy. All this, mind you, is taking place in the Governor's mansion with James trying to impress the Governor. In a minute, James cleared his throat, looked at us, and said "Men, men!" We knew to quit then.

My second story is about my most embarrassing moment, but it has to do with James. I had just joined the group and were headed for a date in Ohio, and we were scheduled to have dinner at the home of a lady James knew. Well, James and the others started feeding me a line about how the lady was a hypochondriac, and that she had illnesses and diseases that just couldn't be believed, or at least she thought she did. They told me just to take it with a grain of salt when she started talking about her diseases and her operations, and that I should just let it go in one ear and out the other.

Well, I was still trying to impress everyone in the group because Jackie Marshall was a hard act to follow. I figured that if I couldn't play the piano any better than he could, that I could at least try to be friendly and cordial. We arrived for dinner, and again we were seated at a rather long table with four or five of the lady's family. The table was absolutely loaded down with food. I spoke up and said "Mrs. So-and-So, this is the greatest table, set with the best food I think I have ever seen." She said, "Well, it's a wonder I was even able to cook it because I've been in the bed for two and a half months." Trying to be really considerate, I said, "Well, were you ill?" James, who had already warned me about this lady, blurted out for all to hear, "No-oo-oo. She was just realllll sleepy!"

James is my buddy, and I love him.

Lily Fern Weatherford

One of the most touching moments on any of the Gaither videos occurred when Lily Fern Weatherford sang *The Eastern Gate* only three
months after her husband Earl passed away. For many years, Lily Fern
and Earl sang in The Weatherford Quartet, and she continues singing
and touring with The Weatherfords. James believes that perhaps the
finest gospel album of all time was *In the Garden*, released by The
Weatherford Quartet many years ago. Many observers of Southern
gospel music believe that Lily Fern has the finest alto voice in the history of the genre.

The first time I saw James Blackwood was on a Sunday
afternoon in November of 1944. There was a singing convention held at the First Assembly of God Church in Long
Beach, California, and The Blackwood Brothers were appearing there. I remember it distinctly because it was also
the day that I met my future husband, Earl Weatherford.

I had been brought up in the church, but had not heard
of and was not familiar with gospel music at all. Even though
the church was packed with at least 1,000 people, I wasn't
impressed. Then, The Blackwood Brothers were introduced.
Before they sang a single note, I was impressed greatly. They
walked onto the platform in impeccable dress and appearance, and exuded confidence and dignity.

When they did sing, it was a song that featured James.
Never in all my life had I ever heard a voice with so much
quality and such full, rich tone. Later on, I married the
man I met that day and together Earl and I formed our own
group, The Weatherford Quartet. We had a successful ministry of 48 years when Earl was called home to be with the
Lord.

During those years, we were privileged to work with The Blackwood Brothers many times. Earl also admired James so much. Many times Earl and I discussed James, and we agreed that James Blackwood was the best example we could think of as a pattern for a career in gospel music.

James always took the time to encourage both of us and because we both looked up to him, we felt honored to be his friends. We watched him and learned from him, and he was an inspiration to both Earl and myself. Today, more than 52 years after I first saw James, he is still my friend and I am still moved by his music.

Brad White

A native of Joliet, Illinois, Brad currently plays piano for The James Blackwood Quartet. He and Ray Shelton are to be thanked for convincing James to form another quartet in the early 1990s. Brad is an ordained Assembly of God minister, and he and his wife have an extensive solo ministry. In addition to being an outstanding pianist, he also plays saxophone and sings. On occasion, he has been known to sing James' part in the quartet when James' laryngitis has acted up.

In 1967, my parents bought two albums at a Blackwood Brothers concert. At age 2, I would listen spellbound. While I was growing up, it became my dream to travel with The Blackwood Brothers, and I became James Blackwood's biggest fan.

In 1984, Hilton Griswold (Blackwood Brothers pianist from 1940 to 1950) joined the staff at our church, and I was thrilled. Hilton had James as a guest on his television show during my Spring Break from college in 1986, and I went to watch. During the setup, Hilton asked me to show him James' arrangement of *It is Finished!*, since I knew all of James' arrangements. Then Hilton left and James asked if I would practice with him. I thought I was dreaming! Then I accompanied James on *I'll Meet You in the Morning*, something I would later do hundreds of times at our concerts. I found my hero to be genuine and generous.

In 1987, my fianceé and I traveled from Illinois to Tennessee for James' last concerts with the Masters V. James recognized me and we visited at length. He even introduced us each night, and my hero became bigger than life.

The last night, I worked up the nerve to ask him what his price would be to sing at our wedding. Karen, my fianceé,

Brad White

thought I was nuts. "He'll never do it, and we couldn't afford it if he would," she said. But on September 19, 1987, James Blackwood sang at our wedding.

After the reception, we brought more than 600 people back into the sanctuary for a concert by James. My beautiful bride sat next to me and smiled. Near the end of the concert, James did what he does best: a record pitch. Mim still teases him about selling tapes at a wedding!

When Karen and I were engaged, we agreed that I would

never travel with a quartet and be away from home unless it was with James Blackwood. As far-fetched as that seemed then, I have played for James Blackwood all over the country for six years as part of The James Blackwood Quartet. I still can't believe it is happening.

What a great time I've had. I've watched James dig snow out from under bus tires with garbage pails. I even remember one night that it was so cold on the bus that James jokingly remarked that it looked like we'd all have to get in one bed to keep warm. Fortunately, we missed that! I've seen him at concerts pulling on his suit coat and trousers, wondering why they didn't fit—and then realizing he had put on my clothes.

James Blackwood's impact on my life has been immeasurable. His voice has blessed my soul, and his character has been a shining example. The more I know James, the more I love and respect him. Beyond the legendary voice and stage personality is the real James Blackwood. And the real man stands even taller than the legend.

James Blackwood is my best mentor and one of my dearest friends. And he is still my hero.

Tammy Wynette

One of the true "First Ladies" of country music, Tammy Wynette and her contemporary, Loretta Lynn, helped set the standard by which all current female country singers are judged. Tammy's many hits include *D-I-V-O-R-C-E, I Don't Wanna Play House*, and her classic signature song *Stand By Your Man*. She has a long background in gospel music, and recently hosted a very successful TNN special which also featured James, J.D. Sumner, Jake Hess, Bill Gaither, and other noted artists.

I don't remember a time in my life that I didn't know of James Blackwood. My mother and dad would save back some money every weekend so that we could go to what we

Tammy with J.D. Sumner, James, Jake Hess, and Bill Gaither at a taping of a TNN special featuring Tammy and Gospel Music Legends.

called "all night singings" when they were held in our area. I can close my eyes and go back to those times.

When I was in the fifth grade, I can remember going by radio station WMPS in Memphis at noon every day to see and hear The Blackwood Brothers as they did their radio show. As the years go by, I find myself still in awe of James Blackwood.

Five years ago, when my mother passed away, I asked James if he would sing at her funeral service. Although I didn't know it at the time, James was recovering from a rather severe stroke, yet he was there to help me in my time of need. My husband, George Richey, played piano and James sang.

James Blackwood has been a hero of mine for my entire life. There is only *one* James Blackwood, and I thank almighty God for him and his friendship.

George Younce

George Younce is one of the best-known bass singers in the history of Southern gospel music. For more than thirty years, he has sung with The Cathedral Quartet, which annually wins many awards from various gospel music organizations, and which frequently dominates some sets of awards. Prior to singing with The Cathedrals, George sang with many other groups, including The Weatherford Quartet and The Blue Ridge Quartet. His onstage banter with his good friend Glen Payne, The Cathedrals' lead singer, adds a comic dimension to The Cathedrals' truly superior concert style. When Southern gospel music legends are mentioned, George is on everyone's list.

In September of 1987, The Cathedrals were singing on Friday and Saturday nights at the First Church of the Nazarene in Denver, Colorado. After the concert on Friday night, I began experiencing breathing problems after I had returned to my hotel room. Mark Trammel, who was then with The Cathedrals, called 911 and I was rushed to Porter Memorial Hospital where I was informed that I had suffered a heart attack. I was promptly admitted to the hospital, where I remained for the next ten days. Needless to say, the other guys had to sing without me on Saturday night.

So where does James Blackwood fit into this story? Well, it just so happens that James was doing some solo dates in the Denver area, and heard that we were singing at the Nazarene Church. He came to the concert on Saturday night, where he learned that I was in the hospital.

On Sunday morning, as I lay sleeping, James came to the hospital to visit me. He was standing at the foot of my bed when I slowly opened my eyes. He stood there quietly for a few seconds just looking at me and then said, "George, they sounded so much better without you." It was the first time I had smiled in two days.

I have told James all this before, but I don't know if he will ever understand how much his visit meant to me. It was a very frightening time in my life, and I'm sure that the Lord had a hand in putting James in Denver at that time. Just to see a friendly face and hear a familiar voice was the best medicine I could have ever received.

I have known James for more than forty years. He has always been a dear friend and will always hold a special place in this ole heart.

George Younce

Dennis Zimmermann

Dennis Zimmermann, a resident of the Los Angeles area, is manager and first tenor with The Watchmen Quartet and is a regular columnist in *The Singing News*. A former advertising executive, he is very active in the West Coast Gospel Music Association, and is one of the catalysts for the tremendous growth in gospel music in that area.

When I was a 12-year old lad, my uncle took me to see The Blackwood Brothers Quartet in Poplar Bluff, Missouri. That night God "handcuffed" me to gospel music, and later, when I was a teenager in the 1960s in the Detroit area, I never missed a gospel concert . . . especially one that included my favorite gospel singer, James Blackwood.

Now, in Southern California more than thirty years later, I realize that God has allowed another of my childhood dreams to become reality. Dr. James Blackwood has joined my quartet, The Watchmen, in singing for our 20th anniversary! We are sitting at my dinner table having a late night snack of corn flakes, which James said he preferred to do instead of going to a restaurant.

Actually, he's mixing several brands of cereal together. According to Mim, that's a long-standing habit of his.

Some of My Memories

by
James Blackwood

If ever the grace of God has been evident in a man's life, that man is James Blackwood. For sixty-three years, I have been privileged to sing the Lord's praises throughout this country and around the world. I have been blessed with a wonderful wife, two loving sons, four dear grandchildren, and four precious great-grandchildren. I have far more friends than my share, and I have been amused, touched, and moved by their memories of me which they have so graciously shared in this book. I am so grateful to them for honoring me in this special way.

I want to conclude this volume by sharing just a few of the many memories I have over these many years. One or two may be humorous, a few are touching, and one is very sad. Yet, they mark milestones in my life that I often use to remind myself how the Lord has blessed me in good times and bad, and how His marvelous grace has sustained me for more than seventy-seven years. I am still very active, and there still seems to be a great many people who enjoy hearing me sing. As long as God grants me health and strength, I will be singing His praises.

Perhaps my earliest memory is of my loving Christian parents in our little sharecropper's home in Choctaw County, Mississippi. Although our family was very poor, Christ's presence in our home made us rich. I knew even then that it was far better to be poor in earthly goods and have Christ

James at the age of six or seven with his father Emmett and his mother Carrie outside the family home in Choctaw County, Mississippi.

with us than to live like royalty without God. I am so indebted to my parents, my brothers Roy and Doyle, and my sister Lena.

I remember my little mother (who stood only 4'9" and barely came to my shoulder) going outside for her private devotions each morning. It seems that I can see her even now. After doing the breakfast dishes, sweeping the floor, and making the beds, she would get her Bible and go down by the garden fence where she would kneel and read. Then, she would usually sing *Close to Thee* or *Oh How I Love Jesus*, and then pray. That little spot where my mother knelt beside that old fence seemed like holy ground to me.

Then in the evening our family would gather around the fireplace, and by the light of a kerosene lamp, Mama or Papa would read from the Bible, and we would all get on our knees and pray. Although it's been more than seventy years ago, those times shaped and molded my life and my thinking, and I will never forget them. I learned at an early age that if I followed in the footsteps of my Christian father and mother, my life would be fruitful. I owe them so much.

We formed The Blackwood Brothers Quartet in 1934, and the original members in addition to me were my broth-

The Blackwood String Band about 1900. Emmett (James' father) is third from the left on the back row. Nola (James' aunt) is second from the left in the front row.

Students and faculty of the Progress School in Choctaw County, Mississippi, about 1925 or 1926. James is seated third from the left on the front row.

ers, Roy and Doyle, and Roy's oldest son, R.W. When our quartet was very young in the mid-1930s, we began singing on radio station WHEF in Kosciusko, Mississippi. We drove down to Kosciusko one Sunday morning, found the radio station, and simply asked the owner if we could sing on his station. Since the little station was not part of a network, almost anyone who could carry a tune or pick a guitar (or thought they could) could get on the air. So the owner agreed to put us on the air for fifteen minutes.

Almost as soon as we started singing, the telephone at the station started ringing. People were calling with requests or to make dedications, or just to comment on our singing. The telephone was still ringing after our fifteen minutes were up, and the announcer asked us to keep on singing. After another fifteen minutes, the telephone continued to ring, so we continued. After singing almost every song we knew, we had been on the air for an hour and fifteen minutes.

This is the first photograph ever taken of The Blackwood Brothers Quartet as it was originally constituted in 1934. Left to right are R.W., James, Roy, and Doyle.

Early in our career, we saved enough money to buy a public address system. We bought one that had horns that we hooked up to our car's electrical system, and drove around the town or community in which we were appearing announcing our concert. Doyle or I usually spoke on the system, but one day our voices were so tired that R.W. asked if he could do the announcing. He grabbed the microphone and promptly said, "Uh. . . uh . . . uh." He handed the microphone back to Doyle and said, "I can't talk on that thing." This is the same R.W. Blackwood who later would never meet a microphone he didn't love.

This is the first formal studio photograph of The Blackwood Brothers, taken in Ackerman, Mississippi, in 1936. Left to right are Roy, James, R.W., and Doyle.

One day we were driving down the highway announcing where we were to perform that night and blowing the horn, when a man plowing about a mile off the highway heard us. He dropped the plow lines, ran to his house, and told his wife, "Honey, the end of the world is here! I just heard Gabriel blowing his horn!" He later came to our concert and confessed what he had said.

No one was more influential in our career than Mr. V.O. Stamps of the Stamps-Baxter Music Company in Dallas. Mr. Stamps employed a number of quartets and other gospel singers around the country who promoted the Stamps songbooks, singing schools, and other products. In return, Mr. Stamps assigned us to specific geographical areas and furnished us with a car and a salary. I doubt seriously that we could have ever received the nationwide exposure which we did had it not been for Mr. Stamps and his guidance and trust.

Years later, after we had moved to radio station in KMA in Shenandoah, Iowa, we received probably the funniest letter we ever received during all our years on radio. An Iowa farmer wrote to ask if we could sing *On the Jericho Road* at least once on each of our programs, saying "My cows give more milk when you fellows sing that song." I think he was serious.

In the late 1930s, after we had moved our base of operations to Jackson, Mississippi, the quartet went to an all-day singing and dinner on the grounds at a little village called Weathersby about 35 miles south of Jackson. While sitting on the platform, I noticed an attractive young lady standing in the aisle (the place was packed and there was standing room only). I tried to get her attention, and when I couldn't, I went out the side door near the platform and walked around to the front door. I walked up behind her while the congregation was singing and noticed that she had written her name across the top of her hymnbook. I immediately realized that "Miriam Grantham" was the name of a girl who had recently written to me at the radio station, and that opened the way for me to start a conversation. A little later, she invited us to come to her parents' home after the singing for something to eat, and of course we accepted. This began a courtship which resulted seven months later in our being married, which certainly ranks as the smartest thing I've EVER done!

The quartet had a 1938 Ford in which we traveled to our concerts, and it also doubled as our "dating" vehicle. My brother Doyle and my brother Roy's son R.W. were also unmarried, and we took turns using the car whenever we had a night off. By this time, I knew the way to Weathersby almost by heart, and I couldn't stand it when we had a night off and it wasn't my night to use the car!

So in this rather desperate condition, I once rode a Grey-hound bus from Jackson to Weathersby to see Miriam (Mim). I had just enough money to get there and back, but for some reason I had only bought a one-way ticket. Mim's mother was a wonderful cook, and I have often said that I tried to eat enough at the Grantham's house to last for several days! On this particular evening, I didn't smell any food cooking when I walked in, and finally Mim told me that her mother had a headache and didn't feel like cook-ing. Mim suggested that we go to Mendenhall in her dad's car and eat supper there.

I had just enough money to buy another one-way ticket back to Jackson, but I wasn't going to admit that to Mim. I figured that I would buy her supper and somehow hitch-hike back to Jackson. Mim ordered a hamburger and a soft drink, while I simply told the waitress that I wasn't hungry. Actually, I was starving to death, since I had been counting on one of Mrs. Grantham's fine meals. While Mim ate her supper, I squirmed and worried about how I was going to get back to Jackson.

When the waitress came back to collect for the food, I reached for my money to pay her, but Mim handed her some money and said "Oh, no, you don't need to pay. Mama gave me enough money for both of us to eat." For many years afterward, Mim would cry every time I would tell someone this story. She would say "Just to think—I ate while you were starving."

In 1939, we moved our base of operations to Shreve-port and radio station KWKH after several good months on radio station WJDX in Jackson. This move took me even farther away from Mim. After about a month, I decided that I just couldn't stand being apart from her any more. I had already asked Mim's mother and dad if I could marry

Mim, and her dad had reluctantly consented. Her mother said, "I don't know what you want with her. She can't cook." Mim was still in high school in Mendenhall, and we decided to get married the week after she graduated. Incidentally, she was valedictorian of her high school class. My brother Doyle had also decided to get married to Lavez Hawkins, who lived in Forest, Mississippi.

So the week after Mim's graduation, Doyle and I drove from Shreveport to Forest to pick up Lavez. We then drove on to Weathersby to get Mim. We were late getting there, and Mr. Grantham was getting nervous, thinking perhaps that I had stood Mim up. He even asked her while they were waiting "How well do you know that young fellow?"

GOD'S HALF-HOUR

During their stay in California, The Blackwood Brothers appeared on radio station KGO in San Diego in 1943 on a program called God's Half-Hour. *Left to right are Roy, James, Hilton Griswold, R.W., and Don Smith. Standing at rear is Rev. George Gaines.*

We finally arrived in Weathersby, and her dad went with us to the courthouse in Mendenhall to give his permission for her to marry since she was only 17. When the clerk asked how old I was, to told him that I was 19. Then he said, "Well, who is going to give YOU permission? You're underage, too." But my older brother Doyle (thank goodness for our plans for a double wedding!) was there to vouch for me and we obtained our license.

We then drove on to Jackson to the home of a Methodist minister who was a friend of ours. We had a double wedding in the living room of the parsonage, and the minister's wife served as our witness. After the wedding, the preacher said, "I've never performed a double wedding before; I hope it's legal." The four of us then drove on to Shreveport that night, changing drivers often so that Doyle and I could take turns smooching in the back seat with our new brides.

In the late summer of 1940, the quartet moved to Shenandoah, Iowa, where we stayed until early 1942. As the war raged, we decided to move to California to work in defense plants until R.W. and I were drafted. We did not believe that Roy and Doyle were of draft age. Initially, we had planned simply to disband the quartet for the duration of the war, but somehow we managed to keep a group together (with some personnel changes) in California until the war ended in 1945. R.W. was drafted and served in the Combat Engineers, while I was rejected for military service.

The day after V-J day, Mim, Jimmy (who had been born in California in 1943), and I headed back to Mississippi along with Roy and his family. I had made arrangements with the station manager at KMA in Shenandoah for us to go back on the air on October 1, 1945. Hilton Griswold

The Blackwood Brothers Quartet, 1948. Left to right are Hilton Griswold, Cat Freeman, James, R.W., and Bill Lyles.

(our pianist) and Don Smith (our bass) also moved to Shenandoah with us. After spending a few weeks with our extended families in Mississippi, we returned to Iowa. R.W. was able to rejoin us in 1946, and we began our recording careers the same year.

The next few years were hectic ones for The Blackwood Brothers. We were very popular on the concert tour throughout the upper Midwest, and our radio broadcast reached into at least 27 states and three Canadian provinces. Record crowds came to our concerts, and at one point we even had to form a second quartet to keep up with the demand. For some time, however, we had been thinking of returning to the South. The Iowa winters were difficult for Southern boys to handle, especially when we had to try to make our concert dates in bad weather. In Mississippi, Mama and Papa were getting older, and Papa especially was in bad health much of the time.

I had booked a long tour for the quartet in the summer of 1950, and one of those dates was in Memphis. While there, we appeared on radio station WMPS to promote our concert, and mentioned to the station manager that we were thinking about moving our base of operations to the South. He made us an offer, and we accepted it on the spot. My headquarters have been in Memphis ever since.

By 1952, the quartet consisted of Bill Shaw on first tenor, R.W. on baritone, Bill Lyles on bass, and I continued to sing lead. We bought a small plane to fly to our concerts and other engagements, which gave us much more time to devote to our growing record business in Memphis. Too, we were able to spend more time with our families than we could have if we were touring in a car.

In 1954, our contacts with our record company RCA enabled us to audition for the Arthur Godfrey Talent Scouts Show, which at that time was the most popular program on television. We passed the audition and flew to New York to appear on the program in early June, 1954. We won the competition that night with *Have You Talked to the Man Upstairs?* Winning the contest allowed us to sing on Mr. Godfrey's morning show all that week.

After winning the Godfrey competition, we came back to the South to sing before even larger crowds. Auditoriums, ballparks, and all sorts of other facilities were filled with thousands of people when we sang. We were the first gospel group to ever appear on national television; we had several records in RCA's Top Ten; we thought we had it made. Little did we know that in just three weeks our lives would be changed forever.

On June 29, 1954, we gave a concert in Gulfport, Mississippi, which would be the last time that R.W. and Bill would sing as part of the group. On the following night, we were scheduled to sing at the Chilton County Peach Festival in Clanton, Alabama. We flew to Clanton before noon, sang at a Lions Club luncheon, and spent much of the afternoon driving around town with a young man named Johnny Ogburn, who was the son of the gentleman who was in charge of the festival.

Late that afternoon, R.W. (who was our pilot) decided to take the plane up again before it got dark so that he could get a better feel for the short runway and the rather tight takeoff conditions. Bill decided to go up with R.W. since he was the co-pilot, and Johnny Ogburn went along for the ride. Meanwhile, large numbers of people were already starting to gather, since we were giving our concert in an hangar on the grounds of the airport.

R.W. attempted to bring the plane in from the end of the runway which had a rather large hill behind it, requiring a very steep descent before the plane could be put down. On his first pass, he was going too fast, and the plane bounced back up into the air. R.W. was an experienced pilot, and sometimes he could make the plane "stick" after the first bounce. Again he took the plane back up to make another landing approach, and again the same thing happened.

As R.W. accelerated the plane to go around for a third attempt at landing, the plane went straight up into the air, stalled, and came crashing straight down. By this time, hundreds of people were watching, including Bill Shaw and I as well as The Statesmen, who were to appear with us that night. Almost before the plane struck the ground, we started rushing toward it. When I reached the plane, I could see R.W. still strapped in his seat, and I started to battle through the flames to reach him. Someone picked me up from be-

Governor Frank Clement of Tennessee speaking at the funeral of R.W. Blackwood and Bill Lyles at the Ellis Auditorium in Memphis in early July, 1954.

hind and carried me off the field while I was fighting to get away. Years later, I found out that it was Jake Hess, the great lead singer for The Statesmen.

That night, The Statesmen put me in their car for the long trip back to Memphis. I remember saying over and over again that I would never sing again. I also remember that the Statesmen, especially Jake and Hovie, kept telling me that I would; that I must. Because of their encouragement and the prayers of thousands of people that week, I changed my mind.

In some ways, those next few weeks are still a blur to me. Somehow I managed to realize that the Lord still had a mission for me, and that He wanted me to continue to sing. I asked Cecil, R.W.'s younger brother, if he would sing baritone, and I asked J.D. Sumner, who at that time was with The Sunshine Boys, to sing bass. In less than six weeks, the newly-reconstituted Blackwood Brothers Quartet gave its first concert—at Clanton, Alabama.

Although our group would never be quite the same with half of the voices gone which had helped create The Blackwood Brothers sound, we continued to draw large crowds and have success in the recording industry. We even appeared again on the Godfrey Show, and again we won the competition.

I suppose that June 30, 1954, will forever be etched on my heart, for I tend to identify almost everything in my career as occurring either before that time or after it. It was so difficult to continue without R.W. and Bill, and although time and God's mercy have healed much of the hurt, there is not a day when I do not think about them.

I am frequently asked at what point and with what personnel do I think The Blackwood Brothers Quartet was at its best. With all due respect to the many wonderful people who have been part of our quartet, I must say that The Blackwood Brothers sound reached its zenith when R.W., Bill Shaw, Bill Lyles, and I sang together, with Jackie Marshall as our pianist. I know I am not alone in that conclusion. I only wish that we had been given the opportunity to record with the modern equipment available today.

By the early 1970s, my health was often not good, and I surrendered the lead singer's role in the quartet to my older son Jimmy. By this time, both he and our younger son Billy had emerged as outstanding singers in their own right. Often, I have people tell me that they think Jimmy might have the finest lead voice in Southern gospel music today if he were still singing in a quartet instead of being committed to his solo ministry. While Jimmy and I have primarily used our voices, Billy is also an outstanding musician and songwriter and has a wonderful youth ministry. Mim and I are so proud of both of them.

During the 1970s, I continued to tour with the quar-

James and Jackie Marshall giving their all in a concert about 1956. Bill Shaw and Cecil Blackwood can be seen in the background.

tet, usually coming out about halfway through the concerts to sing with the quartet backing me. Some of the younger fans of gospel music remember me this way, and not as an actual member of the quartet.

By early 1980, my health had improved, and in the latter part of that year I helped form The Masters V, which also included J.D. Sumner, Jake Hess, Hovie Lister, and Rosie Rozell. I sang part-time with The Blackwoods and part-time with The Masters V until late 1981, when I decided to go full-time with The Masters V.

The Masters V, 1981. Left to right are Hovie Lister, Jake Hess, James, J.D. Sumner, and Rosie Rozell.

One of my most vivid memories occurred when I was with The Masters V. A few minutes after we had given a concert at a large church in Spokane, Washington, in 1984, Hovie and the pastor of the church came to me with tragic news. My older son Jimmy had just been diagnosed with pancreatic cancer and was lying in critical condition in a Memphis hospital. Almost immediately, I began telephoning friends around the country asking them to pray for Jimmy. I am sure these friends called other friends, and I have no way of knowing how many hundreds or perhaps thousands of people were praying for Jimmy within a few hours.

I hastily made plane connections from Spokane to Memphis, praying all the while. After what seemed an interminable length of time, I was on the ground in Memphis, hurrying to Jimmy's bedside. When I walked into the hospital room, I found Jimmy and his wife Mona sitting on the

Jimmy, James, and Billy in the late 1980s.

edge of the bed laughing, and the news they gave me was almost beyond belief. Jimmy's cancerous pancreatic tumor, which had been about the size of a small egg when diagnosed only hours before, had completely disappeared, and Jimmy's color, so jaundiced earlier, was returning to normal.

I have never known such relief. If there remained any subconscious resentment within me toward the Lord for taking R.W. and Bill thirty years before, it vanished at that moment. As I look back on 1954 and 1984 and all the years before, between, and since, I can truthfully say with Job that, "The Lord gives and the Lord takes away; blessed be the name of the Lord!"

J.D. Sumner is one of my closest and dearest friends. We have traveled many miles together, both literally and figuratively. Not only is he the world's greatest living bass singer, he is one of the world's genuine "characters." And beneath that crusty exterior beats a heart of solid velvet.

J.D. Sumner, Jake Hess, and James at The Grand Ole Gospel Reunion in 1991.

J.D. is so sentimental that he has to keep up that gruff appearance or else he would be crying and carrying on about half the time.

One of my dearest and most precious memories involves this legend. In 1979, J.D. was about to undergo bypass heart surgery. Like anyone else, he was apprehensive. The night before J.D.'s operation, he invited me to come to his hospital room with the members of his family to talk and pray together. I was the only person there who was not a member of the Sumner family, and that is one of the highest honors I have ever been paid. Thankfully, God guided the doctors' hands, and J.D. is still just as crusty on the outside and soft on the inside as ever.

Space does not permit me to pay appropriate tribute to all of the wonderful singers and musicians who have performed with The Blackwood Brothers down through the years. But I am so thankful and grateful to all of them, not only for their contribution to our music, but also for their kind and gracious friendship. I will always think of them as part of my family. I would especially like to recognize "Big John" Hall, London Parris, Pat Hoffmaster, and Dave Weston.

As I write this in late 1996, I am just as busy as ever. I do some dates with The James Blackwood Quartet and many solo concerts. I especially enjoy taping the Bill Gaither videos, and will be touring with Bill in 1997. I have mentioned retiring many times, but I have been so unsuccessful at it that I don't think I'll bring it up again.

I have so many other wonderful memories. I thank God for my Christian parents, who taught me to love and serve the Lord. I gave my heart to Jesus at age 7 in rural Mississippi, and that will always be my most cherished memory. I have been privileged to sing in Billy Graham's Crusades, at Elvis Presley's funeral, and on countless television shows, including those hosted by such friends of mine as Johnny Cash, Barbara Mandrell, Tammy Wynette, and The Statler Brothers.

I am so proud of our two sons, Jimmy and Billy, and for their personal ministries. Jimmy has a nationwide ministry, while Billy is a youth pastor at Hendersonville Chapel in Hendersonville, Tennessee. Both Jimmy and Billy have wonderful wives (Mona and Kristi), and they have given Mim and me four precious grandchildren: Dana, Debbie,

James with The Statler Brothers (Harold Reid, Phil Balsley, Don Reid, and Jimmy Fortune) at a taping of The Statler Brothers TNN television show in November, 1995.

James and Mim with President Jimmy Carter on the South Lawn of the White House at a special "Gospel Sing" in 1979.

Brett, and Britni. We also have four great-grandchildren: Micah, Dane, Devin, and Dava. I am also thankful for my nieces Kaye, Madeline, and Martha, and for my nephews Cecil, R.W., Jr., Ron, and Terry.

My most special tribute is to my wife of fifty-seven years, my dear Miriam, whom we all call "Mim." She has been a wonderful helpmate to me. I hope that when the Lord is through with us here that He will call us home at exactly the same time, since I don't think either of us can do without the other.

Dr. Allen Dennis has spent many hours putting together the material for this book, and I want to thank him for that and for his friendship. This book was his idea, and I hope that it will be a blessing to those who read it.

Finally, I want to thank again all these dear friends who have so lovingly and generously contributed their anecdotes

James singing at a Gaither video taping. Among those listening who can be identified are Glen Payne, Lily Fern Weatherford, "Big John" Hall, Jack Toney, Naomi Sego Reader, and Ernie Haase.

and tributes which compose this book. I have been moved as I have read them, sometimes to laughter, sometimes to tears, and sometimes to both. We have shared so many memories together, and I thank them for reminding me of some of the best of these. This book is a wonderful gift of their love and friendship which I will always cherish.

May God bless you and keep you until all of His singers get home.

At a Blackwood Brothers concert at the City Auditorium in Oklahoma City, late 1950s.

James singing Because He Lives outside the Garden Tomb in Jerusalem, early 1970s.

James and Hovie Lister visiting with Senator Howard Baker (R-TN) in Washington, mid-1960s.

Tennessee Ernie Ford, Hovie Lister, James, Connie Smith, Dottie Rambo, and J.D. Sumner back-stage at the National Quartet Convention in the early 1970s.

James, Hovie Lister, Elvis Presley, and J.D. Sumner singing How Great Thou Art backstage at the National Quartet Convention in Memphis, early 1970s.

James and Governor Jimmie Davis at Center, Texas, in the early 1970s.

James receiving the honorary degree of Doctor of Music from Golden State University in 1983. Also pictured are GSU President Warren Walker (c), and GSU Vice President Earl McMilin (r).

Bill Gaither and James during a break in the taping of a Gaither Homecoming video.

Jimmy Blackwood, George Younce, and James, taken during a Gaither taping break.

Les Beasley, Brock Speer, Rex Nelon, Jimmy Blackwood, and James, also during a break in a Gaither taping.

Miriam (Mim) Grantham Blackwood at about the time of her marriage to James in 1939.

Yvonne Denson (sister-in-law of R.W. Blackwood) and Ruth Lyles Jeffers (widow of Bill Lyles) after a performance of Mississippi Chautauqua 1994-1995 at the Old Capitol House Chamber in Jackson, Mississippi.

Personnel of The Blackwood Brothers Quartet
1934-1981*

Tenors

Roy Blackwood (1934-1948)
Calvin Newton (1948)
Cat Freeman (1948-1949)
Alden Toney (1949-1951)
Dan Huskey (1951-1952)
Bill Shaw (1952-1973)
Pat Hoffmaster (1973-1980)
John Cox (1980-1981)
Pat Hoffmaster (1981)

Bill Lyles (1947-1954)
J.D. Sumner (1954-1965)
John Hall (1965-1967)
London Parris (1967-1971)
Ken Turner (1971-1981)

Baritones

R.W. Blackwood (1934-1954)
Cecil Blackwood (1954-1981)

Leads

James Blackwood (1934-1971)**
Jimmy Blackwood (1971-1981)

Basses

Doyle Blackwood (1934-1943)
Don Smith (1943-1947)

Instrumentalists***

(pianists except where indicated)
Doyle Blackwood (guitar)
Joe Roper
Wallace Milligan
Marion Snider
Hilton Griswold
Jack Marshall
Wally Varner
Whitey Gleason
Peter Kaups
Tony Brown
Dave Weston
Tommy Fairchild
Dwayne Friend (guitar)

In 1948, demand for The Blackwood Brothers was so strong that a second quartet was formed, known as The Blackwood Gospel Quartet. In that quartet were Roy Blackwood (tenor), Doyle Blackwood (lead), Johnny Dickson (baritone), Warren Holmes (bass), with Billy Gewin and Ken Apple as pianists.

The Blackwood Brothers Quartet in 1948 consisted of Cat Freeman (tenor), James Blackwood (lead), R.W. Blackwood (baritone), Bill Lyles (bass), and Hilton Griswold at the piano.

* James left The Blackwood Brothers Quartet in 1981, and therefore that date is used as the endpoint of this personnel chronology. Several members (including Jimmy Blackwood and Ken Turner) continued with the group after that time, and Cecil Blackwood continues

to tour with The Blackwood Brothers Quartet.

** James relinquished his role as lead singer in the quartet to his son Jimmy in 1971, but continued to appear as featured singer until 1981.

*** James is not sure of the exact years for each instrumentalist, but is certain of the sequence.

APPENDIX II

Major Awards Won by James Blackwood

Nominated for Grammy Award for 28 consecutive years (believed to be a record for consecutive nominations in all fields of music).

Nine Grammy Awards (1966, 1969, 1970, 1972, 1973, 1979, 1980, 1981, 1982).

Seven Dove Awards (1969, 1970, 1971, 1972, 1973, 1974, 1975).

Four *Singing News* Fan Awards (1977, 1978, 1979, 1980).

Member of Gospel Music Hall of Fame (1974).

Honorary Doctor of Music Degree from Golden State University (1983).

Memphis State University Distinguished Achievement in the Field of Communications and Arts Award (1986).

SESAC Lifetime Achievement Award (1988).

Southern Gospel Music Living Legend Award from *Cashbox Maga-zine* and the Grand Ole Gospel Reunion (1989).

Marvin Norcross Award from *The Singing News* (1994).

Member of Southern Gospel Music Hall of Fame (1996).

. . . and many others too numerous to mention.

APPENDIX III

James Blackwood's "Top Ten"

Here are James' top ten favorites of all the songs he has recorded. All were recorded with The Blackwood Brothers except where noted.

1. *How About Your Heart?*
2. *Someone to Care*
3. *The Hand of God*
4. *Swing Down Chariot*
5. *His Hand In Mine*
6. *He Knows Just How Much You Can Bear*
7. *His Hands*
8. *The Stranger of Galilee*
9. *I'm Feelin' Fine*
10. *More Than Wonderful* (with The Masters V)

APPENDIX IV

James' Itinerary for 1997

At age 77, James continues to maintain a concert schedule which would tire many men half his age. Below are listed James' scheduled performances for 1997 as of late December, 1996. Many more are certain to be added during the year. James will be 78 on August 4.

Date	Site
January 4	Plano (TX) Plano Center
January 11	Oildale (CA) Northland Assembly of God
January 12	Yorba Linda (CA) Rose Drive Friends Church
January 13	Modesto (CA) First Baptist Church
January 17	Bothell (WA) Cedar Park Assembly of God
January 18	Yakima (WA) Stone Church
January 24-25	Lakeland (FL) Civic Center
February 2	Dothan (AL) Ridgecrest Baptist Church
February 14-15	Fort Worth (TX) Tarrant County Convention Center (Gaither Concert)
February 22	Jasper (AL) City Auditorium
February 23	Birmingham (AL) Gateway Baptist Church
March 1-2	Sumpterville (FL) First Baptist Church
March 6	Rome (GA)
March 14	Memphis (TN) First Assembly of God
March 15	Cottage Hill (IL) First Baptist Church
March 20	San Diego (CA) Sports Arena (Gaither Concert)
March 21	Long Beach (CA) Long Beach Arena (Gaither Concert)
March 23	Phoenix (AZ) North Freeway Assembly of God
March 22	Tempe (AZ) ASU Activity Center (Gaither Concert)
March 28	Bradenton (FL) City Auditorium
March 29	Sanford (FL) Civic Auditorium
April 7-9	Alexandria (IN) Gaither Homecoming Taping
April 10	Mooresville (IN) New Life Community Church

April 11	Auburn (IN) Kruse Auditorium
April 12	Frankfort (KY) First Assembly of God
April 19	Fitchburg (MA)
April 25	Belleville (IL) St. Matthew United Methodist Church
April 30	Memphis (TN) Raleigh Assembly of God
May 2	Colorado Springs (CO) Glen Eyrie Conf. Center
May 4	Denver (CO) Calvary Temple (am)
May 6	Lubbock (TX)
May 7	Tucson (AZ) Eastside Assembly of God
May 8-10	Fresno (CA) Convention Center
May 11	Phoenix (AZ) First Assembly of God
May 12	Amarillo (TX)
May 13	Woodward (OK) First Assembly of God
May 19	Greenville (SC) Television appearance (Channel 16)
May 21	Pigeon Forge (TN) Grand Hotel
May 31-June 1	Cairo (GA)
June 18	Lexington (KY) Church of God Camp
June 21	Lexington (KY) Rupp Arena (Southern Gospel Music Association Benefit)
July 4-6	Findley Lake (NY) Peak 'n Peak Resort and Conference Center
July 31-August 1-2	Greenville (SC) Grand Ole Gospel Reunion
August 7-9	Springdale (AR) Albert E. Brumley Memorial Sing
September 2-5	Carlinville (IL) Assembly of God Camp
October 4	Memphis (TN) Pyramid (Gaither Concert)
December 20	Memphis (TN) Wells Station Baptist Church

For booking and concert information, or for information concerning available cassettes, compact discs, and videos featuring James Blackwood, contact:

JAMES BLACKWOOD
4411 Sequoia Road • Memphis, TN 38117
Telephone 1-901-683-5711